Selfless Self Help

Jacob Karlins

2016

2

Introduction

Some years ago, I started off on a journey to learn meditation. Actually, it's impossible to say where that journey started. I mean, when I reflect, it could've started at many points. It's like most parts of life, many threads or factors coming together. One point where it started, however, was in my twenties, as a young person. I was struggling with drug abuse, depression, and anxiety. I felt like a waste of human life, a mess, and somehow was searching for something at the same time. I mean that, alongside drinking too much with my friends, smoking much too much weed, taking pills, and feeling awful most of the time, I was looking for some deeper meaning to my experience.

This had started years earlier: the search for some deeper meaning, as well as of the struggles. Just wanting to understand, to make sense of the world, seems, to me, a very basic human need. It is a basic human drive. So that started when I was born, just like for anyone. My difficulties, the depression, anxiety, and eventual misuse of drugs, began when I was in my teens. Somehow, at some point in time and space, those two things, meaning and pain[1], met up, and I decided to try to do something about it. I decided to stop damaging my body and mind so much, and start being a little healthier.

I started off doing Kung Fu, traditional Chinese martial arts, first by myself (in my room, very poorly), later with a teacher in Lawrence Massachusetts. "Junior," as he called himself, taught a small group of students Wing Chun, White Crane, and some other assorted techniques. I had tracked him down because I was trying to learn the mysterious art of Xing Yi, "form intention Kung fu," and someone had recommended him to me. I had stopped at a karate school, now defunct, on Rt. 1 in Rowley and asked the head instructor if he know anyone who was teaching Xing Yi. This man was very skinny, gaunt, really, with a scar across his face, if I remember correctly. He seemed surprised, but remembered his friend who might be teaching it, Junior. The karate teacher looked through a Rolodex or a pile of notes, and moments later, found a cell phone number. I contacted Junior, nervously, not big on phone calls, especially to people I'd never met before, and we set up a time to meet. Soon, I'd find myself going there once a week for lessons, to a soccer field where we met up to practice blocks and strikes and drills. Early on, he asked me, "Why do you want to learn Xing Yi?"

He could tell that I wasn't a fighter by nature, or that interested in self defense. I didn't give him a clear answer. I think I lied, and said I wanted to learn how to fight. This was not entirely untrue, I did, and still do in part of my heart, but this was not what drove me to learn martial arts. I was embarrassed to say that I wanted to learn about energy, and I'd read that Xing Yi fighters were masters of using chi, or the body's internal energy. But he seemed to already know that, basically, and recommended a few times that I take a Tai Chi class. Later on, I would, although I was too stubborn to give up and stuck with the Kung Fu for a year or two. I am stubborn[2]. If I'm doing something I don't really enjoy that much, all it takes is someone suggesting that I stop, and I'm committed to doing it.

He never did teach me any Xing Yi. He demonstrated it, but didn't think I was ready, so I didn't get to learn it. Anyhow, that was one starting point. I was still a big pothead in those days, and didn't practice what I learned in class very much, at least not enough. Still, I did start practicing a little, consistently, and trying to understand what my teacher was showing me. (Then, and later, in other classes, I would have the mind expanding experience of seeing someone show me something, even very slowly and clearly, that I could see, but couldn't get my body to do, or even understand.)

My point, however, is that I started practicing something, then. Later, I found a Tai Chi school. Soon after that, I tried to teach myself Taoist meditation from a CD. This happened while I was in college, during a winter break. I don't think I got very far with that, the Cd, but I did start meditating formally, and as a practice. I would listen to the recording as I sat in my room off of my parents' barn, and try to follow along with the guided meditations. There is some connection between the art of Tai Chi and Taoism, so this is partly why I tried to learn those practices, hoping they would dovetail with the Tai Chi. Of course, there did seem to be something mysterious and attractive about meditation itself. The interest in energy and the esoteric side of the martial arts related to that.

Over those few years, I'd had to schedule my drinking and partying around my practice somewhat. I realized that it didn't work to be high when I was practicing. That was counterproductive. Somehow, it didn't feel like real practice if I was high during the session. So I would smoke or drink at night, after I'd practiced (or a couple of hours before, I think). Already, though, I was beginning to structure my day around something other than the problematic escape of substances. Over time, I began to cut back, partly so that I could feel a little more clearheaded when I was doing my Tai Chi, or drills, or what have you. Very slowly, the mind-body practices I'd been learning began to replace the hours of getting messed up, feeling uncomfortable, wounding myself, and often when I got high, I'd lie in bed, this seemed to happen a lot, but then I'd read a book called "The Power of the Internal Martial Arts," which detailed the author's travels in Asia. There were stories of training with great masters, careful descriptions of the differences between various lineages of martial arts, and intriguing sections about energy, about chi, and the many magical things it could do, when wielded by an adept. Spiraling, expanding, the cotton palm, S curves, standing meditation...

I won't go into the entire story here, but by the time I was twenty four, the drugs were gone, and meditation had become the focus of my life, meditation and contemplative study. I wasn't fixed. I still had a lot of work to do, to recover from the damage I'd inflicted on myself, and to address the underlying issues, the problems I'd been running away from when I'd started using drugs on the first place, but it was a start. Once my life had that new center, that new focus, I began to devote the same kind of obsessive interest I'd placed on weed, and acid, on spiritual understanding. I carried books on meditation around with me all the time. I would meditate sitting on the train. I started seeking out teachers and asking them the questions which had been burning in the back of my mind.

Selfless Self Help is the culmination of years of practice, years of searching. It is a course of study I've designed to help people who want to grow personally, and have some interest in meditation. (Meditation practice, sitting meditation, is the most important component of this system, so if that does not appeal at all, this is not for you.) I am a Buddhist, in the Tibetan Kagyu tradition. I hopped around from this philosophy to that, even studying some Christian theology in college before finding the tradition that made the most sense to me. I hope, and think, that this course could be beneficial to people of any background, or any religion. As you'll see, I don't rely on a traditional Buddhist framework, although that influence is there. This book, and the course are what I call "meta-religion," an approach very similar to what's being termed "spirituality" these days, but with one crucial difference: a strong belief that, eventually, one must choose a lineage to commit to, even if one practices or studies with people outside that tradition sometimes.[3]

I like to think that Selfless Self Help is a system that will allow anyone to learn meditative skills, and integrate these with their daily life. Then, once a student has gotten some benefit from this body of teachings, they can apply what they've learned to whatever tradition appeals most, assuming they want to keep learning. Selfless Self Help, or SSH, is a training ground, where people can develop some basic skills. I invite the reader to join me as I walk through this fairly simple set of teachings, and as I recount my own journey leading up to its creation.

Selfless Self Help

Part One

Habits

The system of Selfless Self Help can be broken down into a few, fairly simple parts. (That's one of its strengths, I think, that it's fairly simple.) There's the overall curriculum, the practices, and the source materials. Again, I don't see most people using this as their main belief system, or an ending point on their quest for fulfillment and understanding, more like a hub, or transfer point, where some lessons can be learned, before the individual moves on to something else. There are a lot of traditions out there that are very powerful, and it's my hope that SSH could support and augment them.

The curriculum is in three parts: habits, compassion, and energy[4]. We start off by looking at habits, move to compassion, and then talk about energy. As you can see, this is pretty abstract stuff, and pretty common to the human condition. A Jain can talk about habits just as easily as a Hindu, of a Buddhist. These are parts of the human picture. On the other hand, there are some parts of my take on habits, and compassion, that are specific to this approach. That's a super quick overview of the curriculum.

The practices are concerned with meditation. I won't talk too much about that in this book, other than very general suggestions and ideas, because this is something that must be learned in person. There are a lot of free resources out there right now, especially in the West, and especially if you're within driving distance of a city. Meditation is something you can't really teach yourself, but it can be learned for free, most of the time.

(I've spent a considerable amount of money on meditation classes, but I've attended free ones as well. The classes which cost money are there for people who are really intrigued by this whole process, but are not the only way. In fact, any reputable group or temple or center which offers meditation should offer both some free classes, and some financial aid for people who cannot afford the sometimes pricey retreats and so on. This is standard, and the ethical reasons for this kind of setup are obvious. The practices I teach in my classes consist of four kinds of sitting meditation. In addition, there are some writing exercises which support the process of evaluating your life, and your habits. These writing exercises are included in the book. I use writing and contemplation in this context mainly as a way to get more perspective.

Selfless Self Help

This leaves sources. I use three main textual sources in SSH. The first is the writing of Pema Chodron. Known to many as the Buddhist nun who has written surprisingly accessible and heartfelt nonfiction, she was really the first spiritual writer I fell in love with. When I said earlier that I started carrying around books and reading them obsessively when I initially got into meditation practice, I was thinking of Pema. I bought one, then another, then another of her books, and, for some reason, taped the together by the bindings, so I had one large tome, sort of like a thick Bible. I carried this around in my backpack, reading it over, and over, and over, finding so much power in her words of encouragement, her gentle way of suggesting that yes, life is very difficult, but we can find a way to meet it head on, and learn from it.

The other two are Chogyam Trungpa, who was Pema's meditation teacher, and Tarthang Tulku. The latter is less famous than the other two, which is a shame, in a way, because his work is incredible: prolific, brilliant, and varied. Then again, knowing about some undiscovered gem of an author can be its own kind of enjoyment, and Tarthang Tulku certainly is that, a gem of a teacher.

These are the main sources. I draw on them for a number of reasons, including the fact that, to my mind, they make the teachings of the East accessible to a Western audience, and do so in a way that is not watered down or dumbed down. You may notice that my three sources are not only Eastern in their approach, but Tibetan in their approach. This is the tradition I fell in love with when I started out, and the tradition I continue to be in love with. Although I have respect for any school of thought that genuinely helps people, or provides wisdom, I'm loyal, in my way, to the Tibetans. Selfless Self Help is not some kind of conglomeration of various world traditions, not some eclectic stew. While I attempt to provide a sort of framework, in the form of habit/compassion/ energy, I don't try to integrate and boil down the commonalities of a bunch of world religions. I understand if, for some people, the Tibetan flavor of this program is not their thing. When I sit down to meditate with other people, in real life, labels like "Tibetan" or "Buddhist" don't seem so important anymore, though. There's just a moment, a string of moments. The system does extend beyond the basics of the three parts, practices, and the sources, but I get into that near the end of the book. Those intermediate practices are more of a vague plan than a reality right now, as no one has, yet, gone through the basic training and asked to learn more.

Selfless Self Help

Self Help

I think meditation has the potential to help many people improve their lives. One reason I came up with the name "Selfless Self Help" is related to this. As I took meditation classes, myself, I heard, over and over, that these practices were "not about self-improvement." It's not about improving yourself, people told me, often people I respected, wise people, seasoned meditators. I understood this, in a way. The idea, for them, was complicated, but it came down to a few things.

First, for Buddhists, along with some other traditions, things in life, whether the thing we call a self, or events happening, or anything really, are, at some deep level, perfect. Life is good, on some level. Sages and Mystics from many traditions have actually come to this conclusion, that the universe, or that reality, has an aspect that's beautiful, even loving; not just difficult or chaotic or mechanistic. My point there is that improving a self suggests that things are not already okay. Therefore, self improvement is flawed from the start. It starts off on the wrong foot, because it ignores the deeper realities that enlightened or wise beings have revealed to us. Mystical sources tell us, students, that the world is overflowing with grace and incredible energy, but we don't tend to be in time to this (thus the need for a "path"). You can see this in Sufism, the Kabbalistic tradition, Christian forms of mysticism, shamanism.

Not to say that you should buy into those visions of reality, or that those understandings are correct necessarily, but that, for some people, they hold weight. So trying to improve all the time might seem suspect. For people who want to find better lives, make things better, and separate this in certain ways from religion or the religious life, it becomes less of an issue. (If self help is not religious or spiritual, the complexities and forms of those worlds don't necessarily enter in. Each occupies its own, fairly discreet, kingdom. Praying and jogging, for instance, need not be inextricably linked.) For people who feel drawn to self improvement that incorporates spirituality, to whatever degree, the issue of life being good, a certain kind of immanence, is more of an issue. (These are, I will venture, mostly people like me, who tend to be a little obsessive, and see their passionate interest in everything.) I'll attempt to address this problem, in a small way, in the first section of this book.

Second, Buddhists (so, it should be clear that I'm talking here about Buddhist objections to the idea of self improvement, which may or may not apply to perspectives held by people of other traditions, although I'm betting that this does transfer over to other traditions, other than Buddhism) have a complex and sophisticated understanding of the nature of the self. Part of the big idea there is that the self, the personality we feel we exist through, is not something we should entirely believe in. There's something a little suspicious about the self, or as Trungpa referred to it, ego. [5]Improving not only means fixing what's already perfect, but also fixing something that is not as we imagine. According to these teachings, ego is not as "solid" as people tend to think.

As someone who has taken vows as a Buddhist, myself, I like these ideas, find them helpful. However, it gets a little silly when you go from these big, profound discussions to saying that self help is totally off base, and this is because what the Buddhists are doing, and what many schools of thought are doing is, basically, self help.[6]

The literature of self help, this body of literature that emerged in the nineteenth and twentieth century as a sort of secular religion, is all about finding your way in the world, becoming more mature, gaining perspective on yourself. It's about finding meaning, and finding more happiness, maybe even a better grasp of what happiness is. These are the same things that religion does. These are the same things that mystical teachings do, the same things shamans have been doing for ages. Self help just tries to do these same things in a slight more down home, common sense way, often without the drama and system of organized religion, and with more of an emphasis on results. (Don't get me wrong, I love the intensity and power of ritual as much as the next guy, more, probably, but self help usually leaves this part out.)

Pretending that "our way" is refined, higher level, and the self help way is not, this ignores the fact that both ways serve the same function. When I thought up the phrase "selfless self help" it was as a kind of joke, based in part on the idea that selfless self help is what's already being done by many traditions. The self help part is about people maturing, which is there in every tradition, and the selfless part refers to the fact that things are a little more mysterious than we might imagine at first. The self is not exactly what we imagine it to be.

As I said in the introduction, though, I don't see this as some kind of grand boiling down of the essence of world traditions. Selfless self help draws from three main sources, and the tradition of sitting

Selfless Self Help

meditation. Like many self help books, I like to focus, first off, on practicalities. This means habits.

Some Years

For some years, whenever I could, I would smoke weed or drink or do some other drug at the end of my night. This started with one day, sitting under an old bridge, with two of my friends. I was in eighth grade, interested in otherworldly stuff, and drugs, and my friend had stolen a tiny nugget of weed from his father's stash, which we proceeded to smoke in a homemade bong (made out of a glass laboratory flask, a rubber stopper, and some other odd parts, also stolen). It all felt exciting, secret, and like a great discovery in the midst of the boredom that sometimes weighed on summer vacations. That started me, in a lot of ways down that path, which is not to blame those old friends, my choices were my own, but to say that this was one, of many, starting points.

A few years later, my days had become consumed with the thought of finding a way to get high, and, while I managed to go to school, socialize, and get along with other people mostly, my real main focus was getting high.[7] It was what my mind was most attached to, and if I couldn't get stoned, I would feel anxious and frustrated. What started off as a social occasion, with friends, became more about getting drugs and going off by myself. This habit went for a few years.

Maybe it wasn't that long, and maybe I didn't delve into hard drugs like cocaine or heroin, but it was a strange and unhappy time in my life. I don't need to go into a whole confession of all the details, but I became pretty isolated, pretty anxious, and largely unable to feel at home in the realities of work, school and so on that most people manage easily. When I'd do Adderall, I would stay up all night, maybe doing some art project with friends, or just watching TV, and then the next day would be horrible. My body would feel strange. I'd have mood swings, going from despair to intense anger. The day after smoking weed tended to feel foggy, and my body became clumsier. This was easier than coming back from Adderall, but I would often feel sluggish, dull, and the paranoia and nervousness that accompanied smoking lingered, either because the chemicals were still in my system, or because the psychological hangover took a while to wear off.

At a certain point, getting drunk or stoned went from something that was pretty interesting, strange, and fun, to a quest to get as fucked up as possible (and a way of hiding from the world, because getting fucked up meant cloistering myself). If I started off imbibing and being very capable of talking, joking, enjoying the morphing and strange new world of an intoxicated consciousness, in the space of a few years, I would find myself sitting quietly, among friends, but unable, seemingly, to talk or express myself. I would become frozen, stuck inside my own head, driven to get to some height of highness, but unsure how to navigate once I got there, with overtones of paranoia and intense anxiety. Soon, I was isolated, and my sense of anxiety left me dreading leaving my house to go outside. This, in turn, left me feeling limited to the extreme. What is life, if not a chance to do interesting things, and explore? There has to be some courage, even in minor doses, for anyone's life to be livable, otherwise, things just become too small, and too boring. By this time, I'd managed to get out of high school and into college, but was struggling to feel at all functional.

So, at a certain point, my disgust with myself, and my feeling that I wasn't really living, became so strong that I had to curtail my partying. Also, getting fired from a few jobs helped. I remember one bakery I got fired from, and how I went there at least once after a night of Adderall use, on little or no sleep, just feeling as miserable as you can imagine. Somehow, there was a special kind of rage that goes along with an Adderall hangover. Eventually I got fired for not putting sugar on top of the pies when I baked them. I guess my work there, overall, was pretty lackluster, so the pie oversight was just the final straw. You can see how my fun times were impacting my life, and it was this way for some years. I did not flourish, let's say. In some ways, I learned, but mostly, I lived a very small life, a life limited by my need to delve into my own head in destructive ways.

Drug use can be a kind of limiting habit. It can keep people isolated, trapped in their minds, unable to do the things that will make them feel alive. It might be hard to convey this to people who've never had a drug problem, or who've never experimented with drugs, but overuse can often make your mind very unsteady. Confusion and a lack of clarity can become common as a drug taker becomes at home in a world of being under the influence. This is not true of just illegal substances, but really any substance with a strong effect on the mind, such as coffee and alcohol. (Let me also interject that I'm not taking a definite stand here in terms of sobriety. It's a personal decision, and one that I had to navigate, and continue to navigate.)

My point about the lack of clarity is that drug abuse can create confusion in the mind of the abuser, and, in turn, this confusion makes it difficult to communicate, and think clearly. Without being able to communicate well, the world of others tends to be cut off. Hundreds of times, I would estimate, I sat, in a haze of euphoria, with friends, often friends I had nothing really in common with, unable to talk, unable to connect. After some time of going through what really seemed like a hellish antisocial torture, I found myself getting high more and more alone, socializing less (not realizing, then, that finding people I actually wanted to hang out with, and finding positive ways to be alone with myself might go farther towards solving the problem). My issue, at that time, in one sense, was one of understanding loneliness, how to be alone properly, and still be reasonably happy. I think this is a major issue for all drug users. It is a thing for all people, period, but in a different way for drug users. But, let me get back to the idea of confusion, the world of confusion created by ongoing overuse of substances.

One's own strange, fascinating, swirling thoughts take center stage, and people, the rest of the world, often are left at a distance. This distance can be very painful. This distance is, in one true sense, the problem at the heart of people's experience, and why they search for meaning or spiritual answers. Although the distance created by neurosis and chaotic mental activity is especially relevant to the addict, it's there for everyone, because everyone experiences neurosis, and everyone experiences chaotic mental activity, regardless of whether or not they light up, or shoot up. The most sober, conservative person still struggles with the pain of being separate from others, not being able to fully bridge that gap.

Everyone lives the life of an addict. The idea of a limiting habit is fairly clear, I hope, in terms of a substance abuser. The person is interested, above and beyond anything else, even love, in finding and cuddling up with their substance of choice. It feels somehow safe. It feels like who you are. Of course, it often feels good, pleasurable, at least on some level. Aside from the physical enjoyment of the habit, the high, the ritual of the habit itself is really nice. I'm sure anyone who got too involved in a substance at some point understands the ritual aspects of use. The thing is, everyone engages in habits, and rituals, whether or not they drink or smoke. Everyone enjoys the comfort that habits provide. Comforting habits also limit the enhabited.

Everyone loves the life of an addict, and this is one reason I feel that I have something to truly share with people: the understanding that life is measured largely by how much it is constricted by habituation. This holds true for the guy drinking one whisky a night on his couch, and the lady drinking a nice cup of tea in the morning, not to mention those other habits, of place, routine, dress, speech, and on forever. Reaching a breaking point, for me, meant seeing with much disgust the amount that habits had warped my life, and turned me into a kind of cave-dweller, as opposed to someone able, sometimes, to venture boldly out into the world, and enjoy it.

The Habit/Addiction Analogy- Too Much?

To say that a drug addict is being harmed by their habit seems obvious. To suggest that everyone who has habits at all is suffering could seem like a stretch. Think of all the habits which surface on a given day: brushing your teeth, saying hello to people, checking email, walking your dog, exercising. It can actually be overwhelming to think about the number of habits being performed, because there are so many, and they tend to happen automatically, even a few at the same time.

The idea of a limiting habit is key here. If a person isolates themselves, at a certain time every day, smokes something, or snorts something, and then resultantly finds their life becoming curtailed to doing very little in their room, it seems clear that a full life is not being led. That person is limiting themselves, creating a bubble of fear. It can be startling how easily wanting to unwind a little, take the edge off, can transition into a bubble of fear. I've had neighbors, as I'm sure many of you have, who seem to stay inside their room or their home a large percentage of the time, who maybe even resist opening the door when someone knocks. This kind of sealing off of the world is not a real life. Many do not, I think, use what we call drugs, although they probably watch TV or use the Internet, which have their own addictive appeal. In any case, they have a kind of hard shell around part of their life, isolating them and making them less than joyful.

That sealing off happens, at some level, whenever you have a habit. This is an extreme statement.[8] Let's take a look at a less extreme version of it, first. The life of an isolated drug addict is not that different from an isolated TV addict, or an isolated Internet addict. The world is calling, but the individual resists and creates a bubble of control and safety. I think that's a safe enough argument to make.

All habits are, in some ways, limiting habits, in that habits necessarily create a feeling of comfort and control. They create autopilot routines. These are like "macros," the user determined programs which could be added to computers back in the days of the large old computers I grew up with. I tried to create macros, a few times. It was interesting, you could hit a button, and then do a few things on the computer, which would be recorded. For instance, creating a new document, and then choosing a specific font. Then, whenever you activated that macro, the writing program would make a new document in that font. I remember the

27

macro thing not working one hundred percent, but maybe I never learned how to set it up properly. Anyway, habits create these kind of macros or autopilot procedures. Instead of experiencing and living, we are often running a program. Instead of making real choices, the choices become narrowed down in harmful ways, and maybe that is the larger issue. When we are more stuck in a habitual world, we consider fewer choices. That is limiting. Are there infinite potential responses to a given situation? I don't know, but most of the time, were choosing from only a few, and these responses are, themselves, often very stale, based on conditioning that helps neither ourselves nor others.

When I eat breakfast, it can be easy to tune out, rush through it, and not even really eat. My habit of eating the same thing, or maybe of planning my day, or overthinking, have limited my experience of breakfast. Breakfast may or may not be amazing, but, at least, it's worth actually experiencing every once in a while. It might be interesting to taste the food, see the tea coloring the water, hear the water running in the sink. It might be awful. Of course, if it is purely awful, that might be worth seeing too. Maybe the limited autopilot quality of it was covering up some things that should be paid attention to. This might not mean an overhaul of one's life; it could mean trying a new brand of tea. Or, conversely, it could, in fact, mean a total overhaul.

One thing I want to get across is the depth of most people's addiction. I have to be careful, because I don't know everybody, and whenever you make a blanket statement like this, it tends to come back to haunt you. There are always exceptions and complexities. At the same time, I have seen from experience that I, and most people, are stuck, a lot of the time, in patterns of action. Although it might be fun, the suggestion is not that we should all train ourselves to become impulsive improvisers, people who follow whim after whim. The suggestion is that running on autopilot so much of the time limits choices, and cuts us off from direct experiences. This path of training is for people who want a wider range of choices, and more direct experience.

Selfless Self Help

Self Help, the Issue, and Trungpa

One thing that appeals to me, and seems like a crossover point between self help and mysticism is the presentation of the problem of existence. Self help presumes a problem. In "Awaken the Giant Within," self help guru Anthony Robbins talks about his transition from a normal, struggling individual to someone with a degree of mastery, as he calls it, and success. The "before" sounds something like this: he was broke, fat, and had no sense of purpose. Now, as we know, he is rich, driven, successful. In "The Art of Extreme Self Care," Cheryl Richardson plots out a similar problem. She was successful in many ways, but felt unsatisfied, troubled, in others. Unlike Robbins, she'd found some success, but had no time for herself, no time to take care of herself. What is the most popular story in American TV and movies? The underdog. Self help literature often draws us in with an underdog story (and implies, or outright states, that we, too, could be similar heroes in our lives).

Although Robbins' story is more the story of someone just starting out, and struggling to find his way, while Richardson's story is more that of someone who's already found some success, struggling to refine her purpose, the underlying theme is there.

Their lives had a major problem, an issue. There seems to be a sense of "lostness" as Buddhist teacher Tarthang Tulku calls it. Of course, their work goes on to outline, in different ways, how they got from lostness to foundness, and how their readers can as well. It is not insignificant that both angles, total failure, or the place of troubled success, provide ways in, so to speak, ways to approach the path. Other self help authors provide similar failure to success stories (and it is assumed that, at least in some respects, readers will identify with the failure part, and hope they can reach the success part through reading and following the book or books). Robbins' story of the underdog who finds a way to win is more iconically American, but both have truth to them, and an appeal to them, and both may speak to slightly different audiences. What is the same is that both styles speak to a problem, which is essentially universal, that of pain, or lostness.

Chogyam Trungpa, in his book *Shambhala, Sacred Path of the Warrior*, explains the problem in terms of what he calls the "cocoon." The cocoon is a way of being or a state in which he person lives bound by old habits, fear, hesitation. There is a great deal of doubt, not in the sense of skepticism, which is usually very healthy, but doubt in the sense of holding back, resisting life, resisting life in the manner of resisting doing what would really

bring discovery and satisfaction. Since I'll be referring to
Shambhala quite a bit, I'd like to give someone of an overview
before moving on to a hashing out of what cocoon is, how it
works, and how it relates to the problematizing I was talking about
with Robbins and Richardson (and really, most self help writers).

Trungpa's Shambhala is a work that is poetic, very logically
constructed, difficult, and down to earth at the same time. In this
work, Trungpa discusses what he calls "basic goodness," which has
something to do with the view of the world as beautiful, functional,
and full of potential. In many systems of thought, the world is seen
as either neutral, or negative. The idea of original sin could be
construed as the latter. (I'm sure many Christians would disagree,
though, that life itself is inherently bad, even if they believe in
original sin. My aim here is not to quibble with Christianity, and I
have respect for the Christian way, in all its diversity. I do disagree
with the idea of original sin, in itself, however.) It is easier to see
basic goodness when things are more or less calm, in moments
when things perhaps slow down. If you've had a seat in your
backyard, or on your patio, at the end of a long day, and relaxed,
looking out at the area you live in, that kind of being present, being
okay with what's happening, is one way of seeing basic goodness.
Probably, in those moments, which may not last that long, worries,

complaints, memories, continue to play like a TV show in your mind. Trungpa talks about realizing that really, there is no complaint.

This is hugely challenging for me, most of the time. A sense of complaint and resentment is never too far away. I think I understand, on some level, what he is talking about, though. In those calmer moments, which are not the only good ones, but in those calmer moments, it can be a little more possible to see that the agitation of tumultuous thoughts is not the only story, not the most important thing. I mention the example of a moment of peaceful reflection, which is a kind of bliss in itself, because it's a little easier to see life as good, but this is not the whole idea of basic goodness, just one way to find a door to it. It is vital that the sense of electric story, of worry, hate, hope, which so often dominates people's lives, takes some greater perspective here. The point is not just that, in a moment of doing nothing, we can regain positive perspective, but also that this positive and realistic perspective has much to do with becoming less electrified by those charged ideas. To put it another way, ideas are just ideas, not life. Life itself is not defined by ideas, and a sense of life's goodness becomes a real possibility when concepts are handled properly.

Selfless Self Help

With basic goodness as a kind of foundation, in <u>Shambhala</u>, we move on to a discussion of meditation, and all throughout, the importance of a larger vision, beyond the merely personal, is highlighted. This book is not only about personal transformation or learning, it's also about societal transformation. As it is a book about warrriorship, which the title makes clear, it should be no surprise that fear is also discussed. Trungpa's presentation of fear is brilliant, and worth reading, but without going into that too much, the book then moves on to three things: Great Eastern Sun, Setting Sun, and cocoon. Great Eastern Sun is like a bigger version of basic goodness. If basic goodness is the realization that life, in spite of massive problems and unpleasantness and hurt, has also incredible rewards, beauty and potential, Great Eastern Sun is the incorporation of that into daily life. It's never enough to have some good ideas about philosophy or life. Everyone has had those. I remember having a lot of those in high school and college, and they usually didn't help very much. Those good ideas need to be applied. They need to be plugged into life.

If Great Eastern Sun is about goodness on a larger level, plugged into life as a whole, its opposite is the Setting Sun. Setting Sun is a way of seeing life and living life that is essentially negative. We've all been there, so don't take it as a personal attack when I describe it. It's about fearing death, and fearing the negative parts of life. It's about trying to escape, and to entertain and indulge oneself. When people complain about the consumer culture side of Christmas, how Christmas should be about love and comradery, when it has become about buying stuff, this is a good example of Setting Sun.[9] So there's a contrast set up between living a life that is infused with the sacred, and living a life that is based on trying to indulge.

The cocoon is one way Setting Sun plays itself out. If this negative way of life has a lot to do with fear, then we create a cocoon to allay that fear. This insulation is made of habits. Going back to the example of sitting on a porch and reflecting, peacefully, one thing that is lessened is fear, there. In moments when we're able to slow down enough to face things, with at least some sliver of calm, some sliver of groundedness, life's goodness can shine again. One opposite of this would be a lifestyle of total rushing, which is total anxiety for most, a pervasive subtle fear. The cocoon is created to shield the heart and mind against fear and pain.

When we are afraid of waking up and afraid of experience our own fear, we create a cocoon to shield ourselves from the vision of the Great Eastern Sun. We prefer to hide in our own personal caves and jungles. When we hide from the world in this way, we feel secure. We may think that we have quieted our fear, but we are actually making ourselves numb with fear. We surround ourselves with our own familiar thoughts, so that nothing sharp or painful can touch us. We are so afraid of our own fear that we deaden our hearts.

The way of cowardice is to embed ourselves in this cocoon, in which we perpetuate our habitual patterns. When we are constantly recreating our basic patterns of behavior and thought, we never have to leap into fresh air, or onto fresh ground. Instead, we wrap ourselves in our own dark environment, where our only companion is the smell of our own sweat. (51-2)

Just like self help guides, Shambhala offers a story of what is wrong with life. There are different ways of defining it, and the definition of the problem has tons to do with the specific angle of the self help teacher. For Robbins, it seems to be about changing habits, mastery, and confidence. For Richardson, it's more about organizing your life so that the important things have enough space, and taking care of yourself. Both place some importance on physical health. Other authors of this sort place more emphasis on a religious style, communication, or goals. Trungpa couches his argument more in terms of fear, while at the same time including a societal vision of the process.

I have found the Shambhala approach very helpful, personally, and looking at the workings of cocoon has been a revelatory experience for years, now. Once you see it in yourself, you see it in others.

You can see it, too, on a larger scale. Moving forward, I will use cocoon as a handy way of talking about the problem of habits.

A little bit ago I mentioned the idea of addiction as something everyone experiences in some fashion. This is the idea of cocoon. When I was misusing drugs every day, I would not only take drugs, but I would suffer the confusion that goes along with an untrained mind. Overall, my life was not spontaneous. As the quote said, I was surrounding myself by familiar thoughts. I craved newness, fun, enjoyment, satisfaction, but at the same time, created situations of rote repetition. I think in many lives, there's that constant push and pull between the desire for fresh experiences of the moment, and the desire for structure (which gets corrupted in the cocoon). So the problem is becoming a little more clear, I hope. As Trungpa writes, it has a lot to do with "habitual patterns."

This is something you can see in movies and television. The uptight person who fears change, but is also unsatisfied with the constriction of their life is a cliche at this point. It's a kind of movie, in America, in which the uptight person meets someone who's wild and free, or finds themselves in a circumstance that pushes them towards change, they go through some kind of transformation, and the story is finished. They become more alive.

Selfless Self Help

Maybe, if it's a single wild character who introduces the change, the staid character balances him out, so it's a mutual learning or balancing that happens. The wild chaos invoker, once it's seen that he is not happy either, in his life of instability or selfishness, learns something about moderation.

One of my favorite TV shows from when I was younger was "Northern Exposure." Part of the premise that a young doctor, Joel Fleischman, is sent to a remote town in Alaska as part of a program to finance his education. He has constant difficulty coping with his new home, and the people who live there. Most of the residents are eccentric. The way the place functions goes against his ideas of order and the way things should run. His secretary is inscrutable. His love interest is difficult, headstrong, and loves to push his buttons. Slowly, over years, his rough edges and expectations begin to be worn away by community life. By the end of the show, he has finally come to terms with this, and become something like a Zen master or an enlightened person. This story, the story of going from uptightness to confidence, shows up again and again in American culture. There are any number of examples. I could be wrong, but I think there's even a subgenre that is a kind of Romantic Comedy, on which the male lead has to overcome his uptightness in order to win the heart of his lady, who also happens

to be the invoker of chaos, the teacher of how to go past holding
back.

I think it's strangely interesting that these movies and TV shows
are so popular, that they hold so much power to certain people (and
not a small number of people). I would bet that the same people
who enjoy these movies identify with the person who is trapped in
a life of conformity or roteness, and don't usually break out of this
trap themselves. Watching the entertainment can become a
substitute for actually living out the fantasy, which, in this case, is
what people should be doing. By living the fantasy I don't mean
moving to Alaska, necessarily, although there's nothing wrong with
Alaska. I mean finding ways to realize change in their own lives, to
become that character who's broken through in their own lives.
They need to get from the before character to the after character.

This is, of course, the cocoon. As I'll go into momentarily, Tarthang
Tulku has his own way of describing this problem. For Trungpa
Rinpoche, the reasons for the cocoon's existence are complex, and
he spends quite a good deal of time building up to it in his book.
For him, fear is a major component of this problem. I don't
disagree, but I also don't focus on it as much as the Shambhala
approach does. What I will say is this: it takes courage to begin

cutting open the cocoon and trying new things in life, whatever the causes of the cocoon might be. Think of it this way: if getting out of the cocoon was not scary, if it did not involve real fear, it would be easy, and everyone would do it. Few people actually take this path, unfortunately. If someone is interested in this process, the next step is to understand the makeup of the cocoon, habitual patterns. Habits are an interesting thing.

There are good, neutral, and bad habits. Habits extend past just physical actions to the realm of emotions, thoughts, reactions, and ways of seeing the world. I see anything we have some agency over, that repeats, as a habit. You could take this to a logical extreme, but don't. I'm not saying a heartbeat is a habit. I mean the way you talk, dress, see others, eat, work, all involve habits.

Some habits are common sense, like brushing your teeth. Some have a clear negative component, like smoking cigarettes. Some seem very positive, like contributing money to a good cause on a regular basis. Others seem so neutral as to be almost invisible, like the rhythms of speech we use, or the way we hold a book. If someone points them out to us, it can feel embarrassing, surprising, or it can shake you up in a quiet way; so much of our world is woven out of habitual stuff, and yet we are so unaware of it. It seems to make sense, then, that life can get very dull as a result. Of course life woven through with habit can be dull or not free: that kind of living is not even awake. And still, if someone teases you about some tic or overused way of talking, it's so easy to get upset, or maybe to just barely cover up our annoyance with a show of self deprecation, humor, or stoicism. Nobody likes to be called a robot, directly or in some indirect way, but, for too many people, this is life, roboticism.

My point, which I've probably driven into the ground, is that, just like everyone experiences addiction, everyone is, in some ways, like the before character in the stories I've mentioned. They are "cocooners." The life of being stuck in repetition is not unknown to most people. It's also not the only way. I think other ways are possible. It's not easy, as I've experienced this change starting to take place, but it is possible, and worth some effort. All habits, even neutral and good ones, because of their autopilot quality, are somewhat problematic. The habitual quality itself is something to be worked on. While good habits should not be abandoned per se, and neutral habits need not be feared, all habits need to be viewed from a certain perspective, and certain remedies need to be applied, if we are going to "wake up," or live a full life. This is the work on the cocoon.

41

There are two reasons to put effort into hacking through the cocoon and finding some freedom: to live, and to solve problems. Just to live is a good goal, and I've talked about this already a little. Basic goodness should spring to mind, at this moment. Being on autopilot is anathema to being present, and being truly alive doesn't happen without being able to be present. It doesn't happen when routine has dulled the senses, and it doesn't happen when we're on autopilot. Solving problems is the other side of this, the issue of cocoon. It's more practical, in some ways. Everyone experiences problems, from very minor to large ones, in their lives, and it can be easy to try the same solutions again and again, even in spite of seeing those old strategies fail. That repetition is addictive. That repetition is most certainly part of the cocoon. In order to solve problems we experience time and time again, it can be useful to step out of this shell, which hearkens back to Robbins and Richardson, to self help. As I see it, a big element in the Self Help movement is the effort to apply effective strategies to common problems, with results always at the forefront. Results are not the only thing, but they do have some weight to them with regards to the two goals of living and solving problems. It is not too difficult to see when results are manifesting (and I don't mean to use this term in some metaphysical or new age way here, I just use it to mean appearing) when it comes to living, and problem solving. Your life can start to become more present, and recurring problems can gradually stop recurring in the same ways.

Selfless Self Help

Good habits, bad habits

The closed down, robotic side of habits is clear enough at this point. One reasonable objection would go like this: aren't good habits good, even if they are still habits? The short answer is yes. Of course there are good habits. There are good, neutral, and bad habits, and it's largely up to the individual to decide where their actions lie on this continuum. Things like attending to your health with diet and exercise, learning about subjects you find interesting, and doing work that you don't hate are things that benefit you, and seem positive. I am not suggesting that anyone should stop eating healthy food or stop working because these things are repetitive. They are repetitive, however, this you can see.

There are also habits involving others more, like being virtuous. This is very broad, and I'd like to leave it that way. Everyone, whether religious or not, whether spiritual or not, has some sense of personal morality or ethics. Being kind to others is pretty generally accepted as virtuous, so let's take that as an example. Being kind is a habit, in a way. The more you do it, the easier it gets. For some people it is more natural than others. I have become a little kinder over the years. Maybe I've just gotten worn down by work and life, but I like to think that I've made some choices that have supported becoming kinder. My point is that it wasn't totally natural to me, but I tried, both to restrain myself when I was feeling cruel or angry, and to reach out to others in positive ways, and over time, it became a habit. So there are all sorts of habits, and they can involve oneself, or others. That's a somewhat arbitrary distinction. All actions involve both, always, because everything in life is interconnected, and all actions have repercussions that echo outward, implicating both self and other. Still, for the sake of simplicity and to avoid unnecessary hashing out of details, it's fair to make the distinction between habits that are more self directed, and habits that are more other directed.

In this system, Selfless Self Help, I focus more on negative habits, and the negative background of habits (the cocoon). When it comes to positive habits, I don't worry too much. Do them, if you find a chance. Appreciate yourself, and don't be too hard on yourself, which is possible when you focus on addressing the robotic side of habits. This is a gentle approach. It's not like some kind of spiritual drill sergeant.

In terms of the three kinds of patterns, the good ones should be kept, the bad ones changed. Neutral should also be changed sometimes, just to mix things up. (In fact, this is true of good ones, too; they should be mixed up every now and then just to keep things moving.)

The first target, regarding habits, is the robotic quality of them.[10] Take a habit like smoking cigarettes. It's not the worst thing in the world, but many people would like to stop. It costs a lot, is bad for your health, and so on. It's very robotic, too. When I smoked, I would find thoughts about smoking just popping up in my head, seemingly from my mind. Where has the thought come from? It didn't seem exactly like me, or like the rest of my thoughts. Sometimes, I would find my hand just reaching for the pack of cigarettes. My body was running on its own script. Thoughts and bodily impulses can seem to have a life of their own. If we want some level of mastery, as it is sometimes called, we must see and address these "scripted" moments, or maybe you could call them "interruptions."

If we think it's kind to say hello to people, this can become robotic too, even if it's generally positive, and based on the desire to acknowledge the presence of others, put them at ease, and be friendly. So, with both smoking and saying "hi," the autopilot can be turned off. Those moments can be reclaimed for ourselves.

Once this reclaiming has happened, we have more time and more space.

The idea of reclaiming is worth pausing on for a moment. You could understand it as conquering your own life, if you want, or dancing (a metaphor Trungpa used, famously in a discovered text or "terma"). Think back to Robbins and Richardson. In some ways, they needed to reclaim their lives, from being a loser, or from being overwhelmed by taking on too much. My own story, of getting to far into the world of drugs, and then extricating myself, is relevant too. I wanted to feel like I was really living, not just doing the bare minimum to get by, and then hiding in my room to get high. If this sounds a little like a sales pitch, I understand. There have been so many corrupt preachers, and Self Help gurus, all selling some version of happiness, as long as you go with their system. My system is not the best, or even that original. I do think, still, that the desire to conquer the obstacles in one's life, to take it back from the cocoon, the Setting Sun world, is real. Isn't it real? If your life is already spontaneous, full, free from habitual and ineffective responses, then it is fair to say that you have nothing to reclaim: you have already done so. Otherwise, there is work to do. Selfless Self Help is not about ensnaring an audience completely. I hope that it works, as what I call "meta-religion," and then allows people to move on to their chosen path.

Instead of reclaiming, think of conquering. A good general would not use random strategies and hope for the best. Neither would he use the same predictable strategies, and hope for the best, even if they had fallen flat many times. Flexibility, and intelligence are key. Addicts are not so into flexibility. As cocoon addicts, we will need to flexibillize our minds gradually. Good habits are good. Even they will need to be fine tuned. If kindness is the ultimate good habit, think of how much more powerful and courageous your kindness could become. Couldn't it get stronger, even if you're already kind? This is the direction we are headed in, with this journey. It is self-improvement as a way to escape the cocoon, which means living fully, and responding well to issues that arise.

Tarthang Tulku's Take

We saw that, with Trungpa, cocoon was about fear, and about using habitual patterns to create some kind of false security. Meditation master, and prolific writer Tarthang Tulku has his own way of looking at the problem of the self. (Calling cocoon a problem of the self might not seem completely straightforward at first. I think this is the case because one major function of the cocoon is to create some separation, privacy, and insulation from others, and the outside world. When I was going off alone and smoking regularly, this was certainly how it worked. I felt miserable, but I also felt real comfort in being apart from the challenges of social situations, the challenges of having my privacy invaded in small or large ways, which is what the world seems to do. There is a double edged problem here, that of isolation, along with safety. Many spiritual teachers have talked about the issue of isolation, a quandary that is more pressing for our internet age than many other times.)

Tarthang came to America in the 1960's, like Trungpa, and has been teaching traditional Tibetan Buddhism ever since. He has also created a number of innovations that have allowed him to teach outside of that model, at the same time, including his "Time, Space, Knowledge" system. The latter can be found in quite a few books, which include writings on philosophy, science, history, and technology. There are also many meditations in these books specific to the TSK system. Time/Space/Knowledge is quite complicated and vast.

One way the problem is looked at in TSK would be in terms of language. One thing I like about the way TSK works is the play with language, play with language that expresses fundamental spiritual truths in surprising and interesting ways. There is a trend in contemporary popular spirituality to downplay the power of words. I'm sure this has traditional foundings, and it also dovetails with an American distrust of the intellect and intellectuals. That's problematic. Words can be let go of, especially in meditation, but words are also useful, powerful, and intelligent (in the sense that they almost have a mind of their own, and just ignoring or banishing them doesn't solve the problem they are a symptom of, dualistic mind).

So one thing TSK is good at is using language creatively. First, when I think about the problem, I think about the term Tarthang uses, "constriction." He describes the condition of the self as constricted in space and time. We've all experienced at least a mild claustrophobia when crowded into an airplane or elevator, and we've all experienced the unpleasantness of a too busy day. These small examples are restrictions, constriction, and the sense of a small loss of freedom should be familiar in terms of cocoon.

To even give a brief outline of TSK would take over this entire project, so instead what I'll do is this: here, give just a few terms specific to this view that illustrate the problem of a lack of freedom, and later, go a little more into detail with regards to Tarthang's ideas about the self. (It may have crossed your mind that, since this is called "Selfless Self Help," I might have some bold new ideas about what the self actually is, or some new theory, and I don't. I do think that it's an issue worth investigating, for everyone, personally hopefully, and I like to draw on a few thinkers' work to support this. I have a basic plan of attack, when it comes to the self, and some faith that this side of life, the ego, is sufficiently important that, if we do fight that battle, and use some good tools, good results will follow. So, I don't have a grand new theory of the self, mostly I steal from philosophers I respect, and try to find interesting ways of deploying their work.) On to the words.

Bystander self- This is often paired with "outside standers." I find it difficult to understand a lot of Time/Space/Knowledge on the level of intellectual understanding, but I find that reading it like poetry works well. This means that I pay a lot of attention to first impressions of the meanings of words and sentences. In this case, the idea of a bystander says a lot. We sometimes look at the self as a bystander in life- removed, and somewhat powerless. A classical Buddhist instruction also goes something like this: if you can observe the self from an outside perspective, that self must not be inherently central, it must not be the whole story. There is a sense of distance with the bystander self, and more. It is separate from the world it sees and participates in, and likes to "position" itself.

The term 'bystander' emphasizes the element of 'positioning' that is inherent in the activity of knowing that the 'bystander' carries out. The 'bystander' protects its own territory and position. It stands back, not embracing or embodying what time presents, asserting its independence from the world that is known. (264 LON)

Tarthang goes on to underline how the gap between bystander and the stood by, the universe, makes a deeper connection or knowledge impossible from the get-go. Notice how he talks about the bystander self standing back, "not embracing or embodying." This means that embrace, or embodiment are suggestions for goals.

They are probably not final goals. The idea of final goals, like perfection, being completely happy, safety, is questionable. There are, nevertheless, provisional goals well worth attaining. If we respect a teacher, as I do Tarthang Tulku, it's worth paying heed to the hints they drop, and this is a glaring one. So remember embodiment and embracing (which relate to the TSK use of "intimacy" which I want to describe later on. To fend off any confusion, this usage of the term is not romantic or sexual, at least not in more than a metaphorical sense.)

If embodying and embracing knowledge are worthwhile, and I think they are, then the self as positioned apart from its world is something to be solved, a problem. This experience of a self can become constricted by models. As a bystander, the person can choose between already constructed theories, and maybe mix them together in slightly new ways, but this all does not sound very new, fresh, or original. Maybe originality is a myth, or something not to be concerned with overly, a problem for artists. Think of the potential power of an insight happening in time, though. This could happen as you're talking to a friend, looking at a piece of art, or considering your own history. It is hard to argue with the power of a real insight. It seems to burst forth from the moment like a wild beast tearing out of the forest. It can be unsettling, a relief, or heartbreaking, but it has force, certainly more force than the careful theorization of the bystander. Theories and systems can be very beneficial in their own ways, but what TSK underlines here is the direction they often push us in: less freedom. Freedom plus theory sounds more like insight to me.

It's not only possible to contemplate the bystander self as an aspect of what it means to live and experience selves, but to contemplate this as a matter of time. The self arises in time, as we experience it typically, and thus so does the bystander. As it relates to time, just think of how time feels as you live it. Sometimes, when you're too busy, time can feel constrained or too fast. The momentum feels strong and hard to fight. Of course this is a subjective experience, at least on one level, but there's not reason to argue against that subjectivity right off the bat; think of it as a creative way of expressing what humans experience day to day, a way of capturing the flavors of human experience. With regard to the bystander, the kind of time it is couched in is mechanistic and highly structured, even tense.

"Tenseness" leads to constricting intensity that allows for no alternatives. (Knowledge of Time and Space, 20)

54

Don't you love the play of language there?If you don't, if it seems fancy, or confusing, or overly conceptual, remember that it is in the service of understanding life, and for now, understanding the way habits work in a human life, specifically how habits work in terms of a painful self experience, as exemplified by the addiction I wrote about a little bit earlier. We all know that pain of addiction, at least in some small way, and we can all benefit from understanding how addiction and the self work hand in glove. Okay, so the bystander self, or the self as seen to be less than totally involved and powerful, happens in time. There are also experiences of time as being tense, with too much negative or "constricting intensity." But how these relate is less than utterly clear.

One problem of the bystander is isolation, which we've been discussing. One problem of tension in time is a kind of feeling of being trapped. These are not so different, but, still, the connection is not one hundred percent clear. By using time as a kind of lens with which to view these teachings, both can be understood in helpful ways. The sense of being a bystander, being a solitary and separate self, tends to go along with a certain view of time, at least for us modern folks. This is a linear, very set view of time. This same form of what is called in TSK "first level time" inevitably leads to problems.

We want to live fully, not in a lonely or fearful way, and from the TSK perspective, this means new ways of seeing and interacting with time. First level time is similar to cocoon, but described as the subjective experience of time. (To call it purely subjective is not accurate, but for the purposes of this discussion, it's close enough. Everyone understands that subjective experiences of time do not fit completely with clock time. The subjective experience of constricted intensity, or tension, as moments with feeling to them, is a way of looking at the problem that's fairly intuitive, while at the same time pretty fresh, since most teachings don't talk much about time itself.) So the work of TSK has a lot to do with changing how we see time (and space, and knowledge) with the understanding that, once this has happened, a change in understanding, our painful experiences will shift. In terms of changing our view of time, one major theme is time as a force that creates or gives rise to things, as we'll see in the next set of words.

Present/presentation- I group these together. The verb, "to present" is used to great effect in the following quote: "Time presents both the self and its experiences arising together." (25) Now, the basic idea, that time is somehow a vital energy in the universe that creates, is open to question. The general message seems to be that there isn't simply a self over there, and a world over here, and the self touches in with the world, which leads to experiences. The idea is that both self and experience happen simultaneously, as something being presented. It is a presentation, like a businesswoman would give using PowerPoint, or like a student would give. That's an interesting way to look at the life of the self. With things happening simultaneously, think about your own life. There must have been times when you've had the "same thought" as a friend. Where did that come from? A TSK way of talking about it would be to say that time presented a thought which two people saw at the same moment. Another example I like to use a lot is malls during the holiday season. Sometimes there seems to be a hectic, unpleasant energy to malls around this time of year. Go into a crazy mall to, say, get some presents, and you may find your feelings sliding into negativity without you noticing completely how this happened. If you look around, large groups of people seem to move in almost the same way, like one large organism. They didn't vote on how to walk around, it just happened organically. Time presented a specific kind of movement, or energy. Going into that environment, you can make choices, but you will be influenced by it, at least a little bit. You will become part of the presentation. So present and presentation highlight how things happen together, organically, like a big blob. The wordplay used in present (noun, time happening now) and present (verb, to make appear or to show) is something to look at. Tarthang says time presents, but it seems almost impossible to know the source of the light show.

Not-knowing/knowing- these two make a natural pair. Tarthang writes that not-knowing is connected to a certain kind of "lower level" experience. Lower level experiences or meanings are roughly equivalent to the ordinary modes of functioning and living in the world that most people are familiar with. Knowledge is obviously important to Tarthang. It's part of the triad of Time/Space/Knowledge. It's a foundation, and also not to be confused with the kind of book knowledge most people associate with the term. Knowledge, in this way of looking at things, is not limited to factual or informational understanding. As a matter of fact, there are deeper ways of knowing that, in this system, are more valuable. Knowledge, whether factual or something deeper, is a good thing. Not knowing is, at least in TSK, a bad thing, and part of the reason why we experience so much pain. It follows that, with the self and its habits, learning and expanding knowledge is the way forward.

I did say that factual knowledge holds a lower place in the hierarchy than something like insight or intuition, but this is only part of the picture. One of the things I love about TSK is that it doesn't buy into these kind of simplistic, dualistic distinctions. Knowledge of all shapes and sizes is still knowledge, so while some kinds of knowledge are more limited than others, they're all still forms of knowledge, and valuable as such. TSK is not anti-intellectual the way some kinds of spirituality are. It questions and problematizes the intellect, but doesn't just put it down.

How do we reconcile moments of a finer, more subtle knowledge with the knowledge that operates in our ordinary lives?...

Even the most independent thinkers accept without question much of the understanding current within the culture. But relying on information and assumptions communicated to us by others establishes us in the habit of not exercising our own intelligence. Our capacity to know weakens us in ways we do not even notice.

Once we have learned to accept the 'knowledge' that comes to us from outside, we may find it difficult to question and think carefully on our own. (LON, 7)

Knowledge is essential to this view, as is a sense of inquiry, open inquiry as Tarthang likes to call it, and the resulting finding out for yourself that can be the result. That's one thing I try to use when I use TSK: questioning and inquiry. If we're looking at habits this can be useful. What habits are you experiencing right now? What problematic habits are we in the midst of currently? If the self is somehow part of this mess of habits, how does that work? Is there anything to be done?

Circling around the problem of the self, again, I'd like to offer one last look at TSK, for now. In the book, Love of Knowledge, Tarthang outlines a model of the self. This model is composed of various intersecting selves. I don't claim this is the definitive or best model, but I do think it's interesting. It has some truth to it, and it could be helpful as a sort of lens of inquiry. To wrap up this section, I'll be quoting extensively from a chapter in LON.

It seems that the activities of the self can be organized into five principle categories: first is the 'objective self', subject to history and conditioning, to birth, life, and death. (170)

Straightforward enough. There is a self, and it has five parts, according to this model. If, at this point, you're not convinced that the self is a problem in any way, or that it has anything to do with the issue of habits, I will try to start addressing that at the end of this section.

...the 'objective self'... is the aspect of the self that gives self-identity its content: a personal history and a personality, a set of

60

goals and purposes, a physical locatedness and an embodied nature. But this self... is part of the world 'out there'. (170)

There's a sense of self with a story, a style, a body. When people talk about themselves as being introverts or extroverts, as having preferences, as having hopes and dreams, it's this side of the self. Already, this is a vast area being covered. Think of how many things in your life fit into these categories. How much of you has been shaped by where you grew up, or where you've been living recently? That is, at least in part, a matter of habitual patterns. If the foods you like and the entertainment you enjoy are part of you, and this is always shaped by where you are, the culture of a nation or city, then the way those facets of preference and personality form has everything to do with repetition. Watch a sitcom once and it's one thing. Watch it every night for years, and it becomes a part of your mind, the way you view the world, your sense of perspective and humor. Society gives us options, and we choose, leading to (usually) fewer options, more well worn tracks ahead. If you think about whether you like sports or not, you could be either a fan, or someone who dislikes this pastime. Either way, you've made a decision, and you've been defined. Now you're in a groove, and it's not as if you have no choices, but it can be hard to see and

act on them, based on the overwhelming profligation of familiar
ruts.

Habits create grooves in the record of the self. If we want to feel a
greater sense of being in the world or being able to take
meaningful actions, we must work with those grooves, or ruts.
Eventually, one sign of realization or spiritual growth is having
fewer ruts. We're aiming at real and deep spontaneity. Going back
to the five part model of the self, the first, remember, is the
objective self. The second is the self as perceiver.

Second is the self as 'perceiver', active 'here and now' in the
present. Confined to the moment, *this* self lacks the power to
shape, define, and organize experience.

The objective self is the person we talk about in the first person. It
is the person we can describe to others or write about on a resume.
The self as perceiver is something that perceives, obviously.
According to Tarthang, this perception can only happen here and
now, which makes some sense. The second self is a sense of
perception in the moment, without any kind of concept of past or
future. When some meditation teachers or spiritual teachers talk
about being present, this is one way to look at it: they're narrowing
down experience to this one self or this one side of the self (the self

as perceiver). This is limited because it's not the only self. It can be valuable because sometimes people forget about this self in favor of other selves, like the objective self. Notice that, most of the time, we naturally connect the objective self and the observing self, although they could be separate things. It would mean something if those aspects of self-experience were not essentially the same or expressions of the same thing. It would mean, first, that the self we take habitually to be one solid, defined thing with a clear identity is not exactly solid, or easily understood.

Third is the self as 'interpreter'. This is the self as subject in a world of objects, defining, naming, and labeling: the self of descriptive knowledge, knowing on the basis of the past.

So, if the perceiving self just senses the world, without concepts so much, the self as interpreter is the opposite. The interpreter names, judges, and categorizes. The issue I referred to above, with emphasizing the "now" as a spiritual thing, could be seen as shifting people's awareness from the interpreter to the perceiver. When you look at it this way, it's not quite as mystical. It becomes more practical, and, once again, not bad per se, but not the ultimate, final meditation teaching. Being present, being here now, then, is like a technique in an arsenal of techniques. It's like a spinning kick for a karate black belt. It's not that spinning kicks are the best thing ever, or that they're useless. They're a technique that can be learned and used. Let me get back to the third self, the interpreter self. It's the "self of descriptive knowledge, knowing on the basis of the past."

But we have seen that interpretations lack the power to found themselves. A self reliant on them is in the end only another interpretation.

Here, Tarthang is referring back to a recent discussion in the book. What he means is basically that any meaning depends on other meanings. Any interpretation of an experience or reality is based on other ideas or interpretations. It's like trying to find the ultimate definition of a word in the dictionary, impossible. All definitions are just built on a foundation of other definitions. The interpreter self is very useful, powerful, convincing, but also forgets that it lives in space. It thinks it lives in a castle of large stones, which are interpretations or ideas, but because those ideas are only made of other ideas, it lives in space. This is not necessarily a nightmare, but it is sometimes a surprise. As you can see, part of what we talk about, when we talk about space, is some other way of looking at, and experiencing the world of things and their relations.

Fourth is the self as 'narrator', the self of intentional knowledge... the narrator gives meaning to events by directing them toward the

64

future. The structure of this unfolding remains to be investigated. (171)

This level of self is about desire, dreams, and the future. Beyond the level of definitions, this self makes plans. It thinks about the future and what might happen. It wants stuff, and it wants stuff to happen. I find the title "narrator" a little confusing, because it makes me think of the internal monologue I experience, the sense of narration. Here, the narrator self is really more a matter of thinking and planning into the future.

To recap, there is the self as object (with a body, characteristics, qualities seen from outside). There is the simple perceiver (the self that experiences now without defining or organizing). There is the interpreter (the self that interprets and understands as a kind of closed captioning in the life of the perceiver). Then there's the narrator, or what I'd call the future oriented self (the self that desires, plans, and makes intentions for the future it sees coming up ahead of it). Incidentally, I understand if it seems weird to refer to the self or parts of the self as "it." Partly this is just a linguistic necessity. We have to refer to self by something, and "him" or "her" are just as awkward. But I apologize if it seems bizarre. I'm not trying to turn the self into some kind of thing, like a chair, or a painting. Also, I understand if Tarthang's use of punctuation marks and/or italics is off-putting. I have gotten used to it, and appreciate it sometimes; he uses it to communicate meaning. But I understand if it seems overly heavy-handed or somehow clumsy as a written device. The fifth aspect of the self is the owner, or witness.

Fifth is the self as 'owner', and 'witness', validating experience and reality in validating its own identity: the self that underlies and guarantees the perceiver, interpreter, and narrator. This is the 'core self' whose existence is the key to all temporal knowing. (171)

There is a sense of self that claims ownership of all other self senses. It has a feeling to me, when I think about it, of organizing all of the other parts of the self. This is tricky, because the direct experience of this core self, or organizing self, is notoriously hard to pinpoint. However, for now, let's just say that everyone does experience these five parts of the self, including an overall sense that we own them.

From talking about my past, my issues, to the idea of the cocoon, we have managed to get into fairly deep philosophical waters. As promised, I want to try to bring all of this back to the issue at hand. Is it fair to claim that the self is problematic? Is it fair to claim that the self is tied inextricably to habits? What can I say about the nature of the self, and habits, that is both meaningful on the level of idea, and useful practically, for people who want less pain, less cocoon, a more spontaneous and meaningful life?

I've mentioned a few concepts from TSK: bystander self, presentation, knowing and not-knowing. Just now I've also gone through a short exposition on the five aspects of the self (objective, perceiver, interpreter, narrator/planner, and owner). Knowing and not-knowing are two sides of human life. You can either use and embody knowledge, in some way, or use and embody not-knowledge in some way. People interested in self improvement are people who try to upgrade their knowledge, and who try to be cognizant of the kinds of knowledge at play in a time and place. (Note that there's always some knowledge being woven into things, always; it just depends what kind. What Tarthang refers to as lower level knowledge is what most people are usually in touch with most of the time.)

This is a path of knowledge. That knowledge necessarily must draw on the present moment. The sense of a present with a self in there, somehow, and a maelstrom of sights and sounds happening around it, is an example of a presentation. In other words, presentation takes the idea of present to the level of play. The question of who or what presents is also posed, just by virtue of the language.

Knowledge of life can't exist without understanding the self. The self is integral to knowledge. The self knows, or is a part of any knowing, so without a better grasp of the nature of this thing, the self, knowledge is hobbled. (And not just a grasp in terms of intellectual study, but also practices, especially meditation. It all has to relate back to practice, and not stay on the level of intellect.)

So self and knowledge are (sometimes uneasy) partners. Habits are sort of like the flesh and bones of the self. (Think especially of the objective self and the interpreter self. Also, every aspect of the self, in this five part model, is somewhat habitual, repeating over time, becoming more ingrained and characteristic over time.)

Things must always repeat in certain ways, from words to movements to larger sets of actions. The self that sees itself somehow existing both in and out of time and space is bound to that repetitive nature, so habit goes along for the ride. I can't avoid thinking certain things over and over. I can't avoid walking or breathing in a repetitive way. Because I want to eat, certain habits, like preparing or buying food, consuming it, and so on, are unavoidable. The self exists in a world, or the world, and thus cannot avoid repetition, which also means habit. (As a working definition I think habit could be just repetition that has some intention behind it.)

I haven't yet really answered whether the self is problematic. Earlier, a whole slew of problems, or a slew of ways of looking at the basic problem, were highlighted. Trungpa talked about Setting Sun, and cocoon. Tarthang talked about constriction, tension, and not knowing, as well as the idea of bystander self. Constriction and tension speak to pain, and a lack of freedom. As I stated before, I usually read this stuff like poetry, so think of your own experiences of feeling claustrophobic, socially, work wise, romantically, even spatially. These less than easy times always center around a self, and TSK has many ways of characterizing the aspects of this self. The bystander, always at a distance and defining with positions, is one such aspect, one description (and also seems to encompass others, as a kind of larger self, if not the largest; according to Tarthang it includes some but not all of the five selves).

If the discomfort of claustrophobia centers around a self, what other options do we have? It seems reasonable to bring up this objection. Yes, sometimes things get too tight and uncomfortable, but that is life, and blaming or honing in on the self might seem a little bit like picking any random part of life and saying the answer lies there. Why not choose health, perfect that, and see what happens? Why not look at our relationships, understand fully our issues, and let this solve life's problems on some deep level? Well, yes and no. Sure, you could try those, and maybe make some decent progress improvement-wise. But these strategies still miss the self, hiding under the surface. It is always there. It follows, then, that addressing its problems would lead, gradually, to real significant change. Who is in pain? The self. Who is afraid? The self. Who allows itself to be systematically and destructively confused?

Trungpa talks about cocoon, and cocoon as being mired in the caves and jungles of habitual patterns. My argument here should come as no surprise. The inability or, at least difficulty, when it comes to doing new things, getting out of the comfort zone, removing the armor, as Pema Chodron likes to say, is centered on the self. Remember Tarthang's description of the bystander self as defending territory. Initially, reading this, I thought of ideas and theories being defended, particularly as a way of confirming the self's understanding of its world, but think of it as a more general defensiveness against life. This is the cocoon, and the isolation inherent in both models is clear. This is a good way to look at how problematic self is: a deep isolation that is both emotionally deadening and deadening to the fully, vibrant, knowing living of a life. This self is like the unhappy wallflower at party. That is why the self is problematic. Whether you call it the Setting Sun world, or the constricted, tense life of a bystander self, it happens in time, which means repetition. This world of repetition the self ingrains itself in is a huge nightmare, but it's also the dream of hope: it is irritating beyond belief, but that also means we can change things, improve things, live better (even find realization, at some point).

The self in the world of repetition has to live in habits. Then again, the self might love habits for other reasons. It might not just be a matter of coincidence, or a matter of being stuck in a reality in which things have to repeat. I think it's very possible that the self finds comfort, meaning, safety, and power in habits. Who doesn't understand the comfort of a habit, whether it's smoking a cigarette, drinking a cup of coffee, or having a well worn conversation? It also seems like habits confirm the self, in a way. How does the self know it exists? Well, it has done these things before.

As stated previously, I can't claim to have any great insight as to the nature of reality, or the self, and even the system I present here

71

is no great breakthrough or original thing. But I do find it interesting and challenging to use a kind of broad angle of attack. It is useful to look at the self. Interesting stuff happens when you do that. I tend to get oddly uncomfortable when this works, a kind of experiential vertigo almost. I take it as a sign when I experience specific types of discomfort when I think or read about some topics. I've noticed this happening again and again.

I find Tarthang Tulku's perspective to be, alternatingly, mystifying, enjoyable, fascinating, and impenetrable. It is quite different from Chogyam Trungpa's style, in most ways, and different, also, from Pema Chodron's way of teaching, as we'll see soon.

I have addressed the problem of selfishness, and have drawn some connections to habit. I said that I would also offer some ways to bring this out of the world of mere idea, and into the land of practice (or meditation). First, there is meditation itself. When I have taught SSH in a classroom format, I've taught four basic techniques. This is not where the path ends, but it is a solid beginning. All of those four basics, as with many other beginner's practices, work to reveal the nature of the selfand its habits. Practice does this more directly than reading a book, although both are good. I have held, for some time now, that practice is particularly well suited to this day and age, and to America, because people in developed countries are usually well educated, compared to other times in the past, and because information (including religious and philosophical information) is very easy to get. We live in an age of info-immersion, so, while the intellect is a powerful and respectable force on its own, there's more of a need than ever before to balance it out. Practice is a good way to do this balancing. Now, meditation is one way to bring these ideas out of the head, and I will introduce two others shortly. One is a simple, direct method for changing habits (and through changing habits, changing and opening the self, or selves). The second is a short writing exercise that asks the participant to reflect on their own patterns. There could be an infinite number of such writing exercises, but I include a typical one in this book. When it comes to practice I can't teach it via a book or online. It is called an oral tradition, although orality is not the main point with regards to learning such techniques, it's about being in the proximity of someone who knows what they're doing. If you're serious about finding out how to do this, you may be able to find someone in your area who will instruct you. If my words about habits and constriction have touched on something, it might be a good idea.

Selfless Self Help

Just One Wasted Day

Maybe we have not gotten off track, but the discussion has gotten alarmingly, in my opinion, heady. Let's move away from that for a little bit. When I was young, both of my parents taught- my father English, and my mother Dance. This meant, on a regular basis, going along with them, and hanging out in the office as they worked. (This meant coloring, and I think highlighters might still hold some appeal for me today because the pens were in jars or on desks in their offices.) It also meant hanging out during dance rehearsals in theaters, which I liked because I got to watch women in spandex. It did get boring sometimes, however. One of my mother's friends, another dance teacher, had a kid who was my best friend for some years, and I still recall one day when I was playing with him, and somehow we got roped into going to one of her performances. I was six or seven, I think, and had been taken to many dance performances by this time, some okay, some pretty dull, especially for a child. I think I had looked forward to hanging out with my friend, Mikhail, but instead we spent the day with his mother, getting ready for her students' and her big show (understandable, I guess, because she wouldn't have wanted to leave us totally to our own devices). So the day passed, and the

74

whole time, my panic built. The dancing was not interesting, I wasn't having fun, and the whole day had been wasted on errands and sitting around during rehearsal and then the actual show, nothing fun. At the end of that night, going home probably, although the details aren't one hundred percent clear in my memory, I felt depressed, forlorn.

I had wasted a whole day. I would not get the time back. It felt like the day had been stolen from me, really, and as a kid, I hadn't felt much power to just leave or find something else to do. I think back to this day on a surprisingly regular basis, and see it as a lesson in not wasting time, or letting unpleasant social activities dominate my day.

If time seems mysterious, in the TSK formulation, this is one very unmysterious way to see it: something that hurts to waste. Wasting a day like that is regrettable, and the fewer regrets in life, the better.

Later, other analogs arose. Time was wasted doing homework, sometimes, hanging out with friends, hanging out with people I could not even really call friends, but who had drugs, or who would do them with me. I did not learn the lesson of that early tap dance performance quickly. It took decades. It is not unusual, at my age, I'd venture, to start valuing your own time a little more, and rejecting the grabs others might make for it, the painful social obligations, the things you thought you should do, the things everyone does. These days, one reason I have more time is that I've made consistent choices about how to spend it, and I am careful about not throwing it in the garbage.

So many hours were wasted in pain. So many hours were spent pursuing friendships I did not even enjoy or find nourishing. (Some are, but I was not lucky enough or smart enough to find those, at that time.) So many hours were wasted, high, feeling paranoid, staring at ceilings, not sure what I was doing with my life, a life taken over by seemingly outside forces. When I would get high, even a trip to the bathroom, meaning risking some awkward social interaction, would be nervous. Walking outside, to, say, buy a soda, would be just about unthinkable. So, having a real life was impossible.

I can't claim real financial or worldly success. I can say that I have taken ahold of time again, and that my life is strangely normal, in some fashion, and that is what I teach. In some ways, the message "do what fulfills you, use your time well, don't live a shut down life," is common. What's different about what I'm trying to do is

Karlins

I'm an advocate of practice culture. Really, what allows for those changes (fulfillment, understanding time, opening) is practice- a life devoted to or surrendered to practice.

A Little More About TSK and the Problem

It strikes me that, even if I have gotten across some idea of what TSK is about, and how it might fit into this book, I haven't explained the TSK take on the problem, as it were, the problem that Trungpa so beautifully wrote about when he wrote about the cocoon. Now, I've talked about Tarthang's vision of the self a tiny bit, and how this might fit into what I'm calling the problem (or sometimes, "pain"). Below are a few more ways that he gets into it.

I think a good starting place is with nonduality. Nonduality is one of those things that is not too complicated to describe, but difficult to understand, if this is possible at all, and difficult to describe well. The creator of the martial art Aikido, Morhei Ueshiba, wrote, "the heart of a human being is no different from the soul of heaven and earth." This is the idea, on a small scale, the sense of connectedness and the coexistence of deeply contrasting things (the smallness of a heart and the vastness of heaven and earth). Another way into the vision of nonduality is to question definitions, words, and ideas.

Karlins

We always make plans based on possible outcomes, for the near, or the slightly less near future. I am in the process of going back to school right now, so that's one example. I hope that this will help my career, and lead to a better life for me, and my wife. I have no idea, really, if I will live to graduate, or what kind of jobs I'll get. I don't know if I will be happy with those jobs, or where this path will lead me decades from now. I just have vague hopes, and a desire to further my career, and get out of my current job situation. This is nonduality in that many people would agree with my decision to go back to college. It's an investment of time and money that will tend to yield more money and better opportunities. However, it's all still guesswork. It is not good or bad. It could lead to some results I like, or it could not. It could lead me down a path that is interesting and satisfying, or one that is frustrating and a waste of time. There are so many factors involved, and so many unknowns. Is it good or bad to go back to school? Well, I'm doing it, so it might seem disingenuous to suggest that it's not good, or not clear enough, but this is how life is, so full of unknowns and complexity that must be waded through.

We never know the outcomes of our actions. We just do what we think might work, and, usually, what's not too overwhelmingly hard. We apply labels of good and bad to acts and plans, but really, we have no idea. Is college good? Is it bad? It might seem childishly simplistic to attach these labels, in this case, but people do this kind of labeling all the time, throughout their day, throughout their lives, forgetting complexity, forgetting the unknown nature of future consequences. A given action, even a small one, will yield many negative and positive results over time. We pick one or two timeframes, and use those to gauge our guesses as to what good and bad, pleasant and unpleasant will be. Those are really just guesses, though, and the coexistence of positive and negative outcomes over time, in this hugely complicated world, mean that all labels are, in a way, provisional. They are just labels. We have to use them, but also know that they are labels. This is nonduality (as complexity, time, and labels).

Duality, meaning two-ness, or the view of things as being naturally opposed to each other, things being defined by opposites, is what nonduality refutes. The suggestion is not that, because things are not inherently made of opposites (good and bad, this and that), everything is one, or there's some kind of cosmic unity. (There might be, who knows, but that's not my understanding, and at this point, I'd like to shy away from reaching that sort of conclusion, leaving things more in a negative place, i.e. this is what the view is not.) It is important to remember that duality, a belief in the rigidity and truth of labels (which are based, by their nature, on a language of contrast) is the normal way of seeing things. It is how most people go through life assuming life is. It is a workable view of the universe in terms of having a job and and home, but not for understanding the deeper truths of life.

Okay, so, duality is the normal operating procedure, and nonduality is more realistic, if a little more confusing at first. In TSK, there is a model that I like, and I refer to it as the "three levels." It gets applied in a couple of different ways in the books. I'll give a little bit of an overview.

I brought up nonduality because TSK, like Trungpa's Shambhala path, like the Buddhist path Pema Chodron teaches, and like so many other traditions, is nondual. Any overly simple conceptualization of things being one way, or another way, is quickly and efficiently dissolved. The three levels are a good way of looking at how TSK does this. The first level is the domain of what I like to call normative reality. First level time is linear, and goes from point A to B. Clocking into a job, this is first level time. Putting a task into clear steps, first level time. Telling a simple story, probably first level time. First level space is also fairly easy. There are things, and space around them. The universe is made of stuff that interacts. Things have borders, boundaries. Again, pretty straightforward.

One problem is that a certain set of issues seem to happen in first level time, and space. Feelings of confusion, being stuck, pain, constriction, being limited, are all first level problems. First level solutions would be knowledge, and this encompasses enormous realms of thought, some more useful than others. A secondary issue is that first level solutions tend to never take us completely out of our limitations and confusion. They always lead to unforeseen consequences, future problems. Think of medicines that have bizarre and serious side effects: the solutions were well intended, maybe even necessary, but somehow they just led to more problems. And then more solutions. More problems. It goes on forever.

One possible objection would be that we need things like medicine. Maybe drugs can cause side effects, but this just means life is not perfect, or the systems in place to test and sell drugs need to be fine tuned. This is not without merit. I'm not saying we should throw out technology or modern medicine. I'm saying that problems and solutions, with this mindset, tend to stay within a certain orbit. This may be fine in some ways, especially since it seems like society is always possessed by technology, and science, fascinated by it, unable to manage it strongly or even reject it when this might serve humanity in the long term. (Again, I'm not anti technology, just wary about how easily it seems to be absorbed into culture, when its effects can be so negative sometimes.) What I am suggesting is not a complete turn away from first level existence, exemplified by an overly accepting view of technology, but a more refined way of looking at things. Let's not just use the part of our mind that is logical and rational, the part that creates amazing computers, railways, water treatment facilities. Let's not just use the part that creates music and theater. Let's find some way to make those parts work together. Along those lines, this three level system is related to making the mind work well, beyond unnecessary distinctions between the rational and the irrational, or between art and science.

The first level is something we're all familiar with. It is very useful for practical functions, in many ways, but seems to have built in limitations, and can be unsatisfying. The second level moves toward the realm of the mystical or magical. The idea is not that we want the world to be more magical, and we believe, then, in something to make ourselves feel some kind of excitement, but that if we look, there are times when the world does strange things, magical things. Whether this is more about our perceptions, or more about the world itself is not something I'm especially interested in fiddling around with, since those two things always go together (the notable exception being, clearly, when someone is crazy, then it is a matter of perception skewing reality). Anyway, second level things go beyond first level ideas about discretion. Second level time is more about momentum, things happening in ways that are not completely linear. Second level space is about looking at the borders of things, the structures of things, and examining. What you find is usually more space, or what Tarthang calls "structured space." Although this fits easily with certain kinds of scientific theory, it is easily ignored or forgotten by most people, even if they claim to believe in science. A chair is made of space, but we experience it and think of it and talk about it as "chair." Second level knowledge attempts to break through the limitations, patterns, and structures of first level knowledge. Remember that first level knowledge encompasses vast areas of logical or conventional understanding. Second level knowledge is about applying questioning, and thought that is not completely rational or linear, to free things up. For me, art and poetry, especially, come to mind. When you try to read a poem, that reading is different from reading a street sign. Many things, including, but not limited to logical mind, are brought into play. Intuition can be exercised. (Not that second level knowledge is simply intuition, but things like intuition come into play there.)

At one point, Tarthang makes clear that, for people who develop their bodies and minds, yogis, various special abilities can be attained. In the eastern traditions, this is sometimes called "siddhi," magical power, and it is often deemphasized.[11] It is not the point of meditation, or practice. It can be a side benefit, a side effect of serious effort over time. Siddhis would include things like being able to use intuition so effectively that it is like reading another's mind (which we've all done, in some small way, at some time), or gaining incredible agility, or being able to create amazing projects at lightning speed. I can't say that I've developed any of these things, but they are part of the tradition, and potentially a part of the path, although, again, not the real point, or goal. There are stories, some more credible than others, about masters both modern and ancient, who could do amazing things. Tarthang equates these abilities with the second level. By training, and accessing one's own power, the limitations of the commonplace first level can be broken through. However, the third level dissolves even those accomplishments. It is worth adding that, although the second level is no end point, it is very useful as a counterbalance to the assumptions, negative normalcy, and "we know what we're doing here" chains of the first level. Each level has its place and its power.

That is, in a way, a third level insight. I wrote, earlier, about nonduality, nonduality in terms of questioning things, things not being as clearly defined or knowable as we normally assume. The third level is where this becomes most relevant. Because the way life is, is best described as nondualistic, not limited to any words, or ideas, this applies to time, space, and knowledge. First and second level time exist as a kind of progression, from more to less limited ways of thinking, but all definitions, ways of knowing, are somewhat conceptual, so, in that progression, they can all be seen through. The clear rationality, the business as usual style of the first level, is not bad, and the open inquiry and magical qualities of the second level are not good. Both are manifestations of the world of time, of space, of knowledge. Both are good, in their own ways. So, third level stuff is really about trying to, if possible, dissolve simplistic conceptions of good versus bad, and seeing how things display goodness already. This is why I said that seeing that each level has its place was a kind of third level insight. Actually, it is more like a second level insight, blurring into the third, I think; it is too defined and rationalistic to be truly third level. At that highest point, which wouldn't acknowledge itself as being higher or lower, even differences between first, second, and third would be thrown out, and the practicality of the thought that "each level has its place and power" would be seen to be too limited, limited to ideas about hierarchy, power, and using levels of understanding to accomplish things.

Later, near the end of the book, I want to look more closely at language, because while habit, and compassion are the first two sections, language is really the third, and final. Here, I will say that one big thing the three level schema does is dissolve language, progressive, persuasively, and carefully. Let's look back at the problem we started out with, the painful cocoon, what everyone struggles with in so many ways. This struggle has mostly to do with language. Now, it is childishly simplistic to imagine that we could discard or ban words, since words get in the way of clear perception sometimes, which they do, or because they create confusion, miscommunications, and support insanity, which they do. Words are too tenacious and intelligent, too full of life and energy to just be thrown in the garbage. We need wise strategies for working through them, even transforming them into goodness and power. This is one specialty, working with language, of TSK. It is also done, in a different fashion, through simple practice.

Selfless Self Help

The Practices

I would like to talk about "practice" as Buddhists like to call it, or meditation, or prayer, as other people tend to call it. I mentioned earlier that I like to teach four techniques when I do my classes. I usually start off with the "body scan." We do this, at the beginning of class, for a few sessions, and then move on to the next two.

Meditation, like any mind/body skill is best learned in person, from a teacher. I can't really teach it to you here, in disembodied book form. I can say a few things that skirt around the issue. First off, I think having a practice is the most important thing. It need not be meditation, although that's the path I've taken, and a path I find helpful. Some people do yoga, or other things. It's important that you learn what you're doing from someone who's pretty good at it, and who you can, at some point, ask questions of, so you can clarify things. (Questions, from bigger philosophical ones, to smaller postural or procedural ones, will always come up, and sometimes these two categories can blend into each other in interesting ways.)

I like to say that 90% of what I teach is meditation. The ideas and exercises are mostly extraneous. Not that ideas aren't important, just that mine, here, don't happen to be the most important.[12] If what I'm presenting is even a little interesting to you, try taking a class of some kind, or just try talking to a priest about having a personal daily practice.

The body scan itself is interesting for a lot of different reasons. I imagine people of any faith could do it, unless they see a good reason not to. It focuses on the body, obviously, which a lot of folks tend to ignore or lose touch with. I think a lot of people spend a long time, when they're learning to meditate, just getting back in touch with their bodies. It can be done well in public, which can't really be said for some other formal kinds of meditation (especially those done with the eyes open; I do the body scan with the eyes closed). It also has a gentle learning curve. My experience with it has been that you can invest a little time in it, and develop some concentration, even a little bliss, without too much effort or difficulty. I can't say the same for other forms of practice. Practicing is definitely not about feeling blissful. That's not the point. However, it can be nice. With the body scan, it is not too hard to generate it if you practice a while.

Selfless Self Help

I probably shouldn't say too much more about meditation here. I recommend, like most meditation teachers, that you start off with a little in the morning, or at some other convenient time, and very gradually build up the length of time from there. Practicing a little, at least, is key because without some powerful way to circumvent the rational parts of the mind, those parts of the mind will tend to trip you up. They will trip up your progress, and limit how deep your growth is. Rationality is an indispensable tool, but it can't cover everything. Not everything falls under the umbrella of rationality. It's sort of like a camera that's very powerful, and beautiful, but just can't capture certain frequencies of light. This is more or less the same issue as words, the discussion from the end of last chapter. We need, as spiritual adventurers, clever ways to both engage and reroute our language problems. Practice does this very well.

I remember, when I started, five minutes a day seemed to create some big changes in how I felt. My mind felt significantly changed after each short session, and some odd things would happen with my senses, too, especially visual perceptions. Another way to say it would be that things got more interesting, and not in some breakthrough-level enlightenment type way, but in a quieter way; things got more interesting just to experience as lived things.

Karlins

Practicing, establishing one's own daily practice, is more important than any of my words here, my ideas, and I hope that you will try it. I have found that, from around ten years of sitting, some big changes have happened in my life.

Selfless Self Help

Tai Chi

One thing self help, and religion, art, and culture can do is inspire people. They can give people a more robust sense of there being many millions of possibilities out there, so many possibilities that even the word possibility doesn't really encompass it all. Now, it's easy, and not totally unreasonable to laugh at this kind of talk- isn't this the same old shtick, isn't this just preying on people's weaknesses and need for promises of a better life? If you've picked up a self help book, or spent any time around New Age types, "possibilities" are something you might get sick of hearing about. So is it the usual nonsense?

Actually, it might be, or it might not. It really depends on the nature of the practices being delivered by a tradition, and the promises being offered. I remember watching TV, as a kid, when I used to really watch TV, with ads, before the Internet and Netflix, and you'd see commercials for get rich quick schemes. They seemed to often involve a man in some kind of unnatural looking formal wear, as if he never actually wore that in his life, like a blazer and khakis, or a crisp polo shirt, and he would stand on a boat, telling you about how he used to miserably poor, and then turned everything around. Then the testimonials from his supposed customers, about how they'd used is system to great effect, and were now making thousands a month, doing nothing.

Those kind of promises are sleazy and you'd be right change the channel. Those con men also, presumably, don't offer good, legitimate practices, real ways to get rich (or everyone would already be rich). But inspiration shouldn't get a bad name just because some people coopt it. I think people sometimes distrust messages of hope or inspiration because it seems too easy, and therefore unrealistic or untrustworthy. The thing is, being inspired can lead to results. Feeling uninspired, lethargic, or hopeless will also lead to results, but not ones that you'd necessarily desire. You don't have to pick one. You don't have to be inspired all the time, but finding sources for it can be really useful, among other reasons for getting things done, and I think this is something inspiration-seekers know, whether consciously or unconsciously.

One thing I like about Tony Robbins' system, and I don't agree with all of it, is that he finds ways to inspire his audience. He is full of vitality and energy, quantities that, in a teacher, do a few things, including inspiring the audience. I have worked with quite a few teachers, although not Robbins, mostly Buddhist meditation teachers, and being around someone with a strong sense of vital energy does inspire you, liven you up. Peoples' presences are contagious, for good or bad! Not only is Robbins vital, he presents his ideas, about change, about belief, in ways that inspire, leading to a sense of personal power and possibility. Self help, religion, and culture can all do this.

I said earlier that I'd studied Kung Fu with a man in Lawrence, Massachusetts. One thing about learning martial arts was that I got a sense of possibility. Watching movies (where there were special effects, wires, and so on, involved) inspired me. Then, seeing actual fighters moving with razor precision, fluidity, being able to read your body language and anticipate where you'd move, inspired me too, in a different way. As I think I've said before, martial arts was really the start of my training, a training which I continue today. I don't really do a martial art right now. I meditate, I write, I exercise. The martial arts have fallen away, at least for now, but I do practice, and train, consistently, and this is super-important. Without some dedication and consistency, nothing will happen. They used to call it a work ethic, and I don't hear that term much these days, although certainly hard work is still going on, all over. But, inspiration aside, my time doing martial arts taught me what it means to do a practice every day, and how this pushes you gently towards results.

After a little time with Kung Fu, I found myself doing Tai Chi. This style was more suited to my personality in some ways. I could do it alone, outside, as a form, and I'd always wanted to learn forms. There was something magical, ritual, dancelike about them. Then, there were the internal experiences of what is called "chi," or energy. That was something I'd been dreaming of learning about for years. In fact, when my teacher had asked me why I wanted to learn Kung Fu, that was probably the main reason. My own experiences of it were variable, but it could feel like a wind, electricity, or warmth in my hands or arms. I knew that I felt something alive and wholesome at the end of a workout, and not like the pleasant soreness or exhaustion that would follow playing sports or jogging.

That was a possibility I wanted to explore, energy. I remember feeling it strongly, sometimes, when I'd walk to my teacher's studio, next to a mechanic shop, waves of it billowing out of the studio. I'd feel my solar plexus, stomach, sort of light up with rushes of energy. It was a little bit like the rushes you feel if you get really excited, but without the anxiety or harsh edge, just strong waves of good feeling, flowing consistently out from one place. Sadly, that teacher has moved, and the studio is no longer there. I think he built a house and studio in Maine, where he lives now.

We have talked about one way of looking at the problem of the human condition, what has been called "the cocoon." You could think of it as the opposite of inspiration. You could call this state "knowing it already." People sometimes assume they know it all already, or enough already. Possibilities of strange and amazing things are just dreams, fantasies. Not only is this untrue, it leads to a smaller life, and you probably don't want that for yourself, or for others. Over the years, my sense of what is possible was stretched by martial training, even if I never got that skilled or coordinated. We are responsible, finally, for where our lives head, even if there are many bumps and challenges along the way. Part of my work, with this book, and the classes I've been teaching over the last few years, is to nudge people a little, to get them to see some new possibilities, and to attempt a larger life. It is a cliche to say, "if I can do it, you can," but really, do think of what I am like, and the difficulties I've navigated- I can be shy, stubborn, irritable, and negative. Yet, I've managed to push myself out of the comfort zone many times, and find some things in this life that have enriched my world incredibly. These are the kind of possibilities I offer, the processing, through practice, of one's both beautiful and neurotic personality, to the point where life begins to reveal some more possibilities, like a tree taking root in good soil.

If you have never seen Tai Chi being done, take a moment to watch it, if you can. Isn't there something to it, some grace to it? What is that? There is some subtle rhythm and flow coming from the body of a practitioner, and in their interaction with the ground, the environment. Think of possibilities of beauty. It is so easy to forget about the power of beauty as we talk about habituation, addiction, and improvement. Those things don't have to clash, but they are different worlds. Think about the power and beauty of strangeness, the weird. Strangeness can mean something is wrong or dangerous, but when it doesn't mean this, and this is frequently the case, that it is not threatening, the weird is the world waving. From the car of overly normal, the weird waves. It says hello, suggesting another world is possible.

Selfless Self Help

Pema

I discovered the writing of Pema Chodron when I was in college. I used to enjoy the large, industrial styled library of Oberlin College. It was made of concrete, and the colors of the carpet and everything seemed to come out of the sixties or seventies, lots of burnt umber, ugly combinations of orange and brown and green. One of the good things about it was the size. Like most college libraries, I'd imagine, it contained thousands of books, maybe millions. I would wander around the stacks, sometimes looking for titles about martial arts (this section was understandably not so extensive), sometimes looking for other subjects, like philosophy, sometimes just browsing. It was quiet, and safe, and I liked the smell of the old books. (At this point in my life, I was intensely nervous a lot of the time, so a quiet safe seeming place was attractive.) During one of these times I picked up something by Pema, and that was that. I took her as my teacher, from that point on, for a few years. Although I read other authors, she was the only one who really moved me, when it came to Buddhist practice and theory.

She has been teaching for a long time now. She was a student of Chogyam Trungpa, when he was alive. She is a nun, and was born in America. Pema now runs a monastery in Canada. Because she's been teaching for such a long time, she has many books (also, she has become very popular, thanks largely to Oprah, who has interviewed her on air). Some of her writing is more traditionally Buddhist, and some of it is less specific to that tradition. I'm not going to try to summarize what she has said. There's a lot, all of it good, and you can read it for yourself. I'm going to focus on a few key ideas, and one in particular that I use in Selfless Self Help, and in my own life on a day to day basis.

Chodron puts a lot of emphasis on being gentle with oneself, and directly experiencing emotions as something physical. These are something Trungpa also talked about, at least the first one. They're both traditional. Chodron talks about "waking up" to our experience of life, our suffering, and our habitual reactions.

Here is a quote from Pema, in which she talks about lightening up, finding joy, and doing something different.

Being able to lighten up is the key to feeling at home with your body, mind, and emotions, to feeling worthy to live on this planet.

Selfless Self Help

For example, you can hear the slogan "Always maintain only a joyful mind" and start beating yourself over the head for never being joyful. That kind of witness is a bit heavy.

This earnestness, this seriousness about everything in our lives — including practice — this goal-oriented, we're going-to-do-it-or-else attitude, is the world's greatest killjoy. There's no sense of appreciation because we're so solemn about everything. In contrast, a joyful mind is very ordinary and relaxed. So lighten up. Don't make such a big deal.

When your aspiration is to lighten up, you begin to have a sense of humor. Your serious state of mind keeps getting popped. In addition to a sense of humor, a basic support for a joyful mind is curiosity, paying attention, taking an interest in the world around you. Happiness is not required, but being curious without a heavy judgmental attitude helps. If you are judgmental, you can even be curious about that.

Curiosity encourages cheering up. So does simply remembering to do something different. We are so locked into this sense of burden — Big Deal Joy and Big Deal Unhappiness — that it's sometimes helpful just to change the pattern. Anything out of the ordinary will help. You can go to the window and look at the sky, you can splash cold water on your face, you can sing in the shower, you can go jogging — anything that's against your usual pattern. That's how things start to lighten up. (Chodron, Comfortable with Uncertainty)

She is writing about a few things there. I particularly like the part at the end, where she talks about interrupting patterns. I'm going to repeat that for emphasis.

...it's sometimes helpful just to change the pattern. Anything out of the ordinary will help. You can go to the window and look at the sky, you can splash cold water on your face, you can sing in the shower, you can go jogging — anything that's against your usual pattern.

She suggests doing something else, as a way to wake up and break out of the momentum of habituation, in a number of places in her books. She also says that the teacher Gurdjieff had his students do something similar, just in order to wake up. I like to think of it as a kind of mental yoga. In physical yoga training, you do different sorts of stretches, movements, balances, that can leave you feeling sore, but more open, like the habitual armor your body was locked into has been loosened somewhat. We develop patterns of posture and movement over time, related to many factors (including culture), and something like stretching can loosen those, which can, in turn, lead to other, deeper, results. Doing something a little surprising or other or out of the normal pattern can have the same kind of result. The muscular knots and forms of your mind can get looser, more graceful and flexible.

One of the first things you notice, if you try this, is that there's something hard to see about those habitual patterns. Most of the time, we are not cognizant of those patterns being acted out, and even if we try to break away from them, the second choices, or the other options we go with, are just as habitual. (Think of eating healthy for a while, then going back to eating junk, feeling bad, then eating something healthy. Breaking or changing a habit often ends up with someone going into another, equally entrenched habit.)

The most fundamental aggression to ourselves, the most fundamental harm we can do to ourselves, is to remain ignorant by not having the courage and the respect to look at ourselves honestly and gently. (Chödrön, When Things Fall Apart: Heart Advice for Difficult Times)

It is easy to avoid looking at habitual patterns. Once we start, it is easy to get negative about ourselves. This is even more true if we notice how subtle these patterns are, and the tendency to go from one pattern to another, even as we try to be more spontaneous or even as we try to choose new options. Gentleness and kindness towards yourself is needed. It makes it work better. Without that kindness, the whole process becomes much more difficult, because we're struggling with not only doing things in a new way, but also slogging through the internal monologue about how we are failing, how we not measuring up as people.

I gave a talk at a library last week, and a woman in the audience asked a question. She was struggling with feeling a lot of hate about a terrorist who'd been in the news, a man who'd injured many people, and killed a number. During the discussion that followed this question, one thing I said was that it was easy to fall into the trap of feeling bad about feeling bad. In a very similar way, with introspection or reflection, it's easy to fall into the trap of feeling bad about our patterns, and then even feeling bad about that! This is a key point to introduce some gentleness, and maybe a little humor. Chodron is big on both of those things, gentleness (remember the two disciplines of a warrior) and having a sense of humor, which make life so much more pleasant and bearable. This master teacher and master meditator has a few key themes she focuses on, such as kindness to oneself, and breaking out of addiction and habituation. Her style is disarmingly common sense much of the time, but don't let that fool you. She is a monastic, a nun. She has studied with great teachers and put in thousands of hours "on the cushion." In SSH, she embodies the feminine principle in many ways.

More Pema: Applying the Idea, and Outcomes

Just like the other master teachers I've included here, there is much to Pema's writing that I have not included. The part that I focus on in this context is the idea of doing something unusual in order to break the momentum of habits, or the cocoon. I read this when I was in college, as I said, but it didn't really penetrate my mind for a few years. I'm not sure when this happened, but the idea of cocoon, being asleep in habits, and trying new things did seem to make sense in a clear, unavoidable way. I started trying it, trying new ways to do things. Actually, in some way I'd always been doing it, but it took on new meaning at that time, and I began doing it in a different way.

The easiest thing is to do something out of the ordinary with an action that is fairly meaningless, like opening a door, or with the things you look at as you walk down the street. (That's one of those examples that I've actually tried, and is hauntingly, bizarrely habitual. You may find a number of these. A lot of times, seemingly innocuous, minor things, things we think are based on interest or whim are very robotic. I found that where I look in a car, or when I walk, is often very robotic. Same landmarks, same areas, again, and again.)

The idea is to break out of the cocoon. I found, as I tried this, a few things. It felt weird, and not just because I got self conscious about people watching or judging me. It felt weird the way it feels weird to try to write with your off hand. It was difficult sometimes for no clear reason. My habit seemed to have some kind of magnetism or gravity all its own. Suddenly actions that were natural became more clumsy. In addition, I didn't just break through to some kind of enlightenment right away. It worked gradually. It was also harder with some things than others.

The hardest patterns to shift are usually ones involving strong emotions and other people. I think that makes sense. This is where the action is, so to speak. Working with minor habits is just preparation and support for working on larger habits (negative emotions and social interactions). Now, I don't outline a detailed way of seeing social life, or the emotions. Like with defining the negativity of habits, I leave that up to you mostly. As a Buddhist, I have my roadmaps, as far as emotional life goes, as far as what virtue is. I think it's a safer bet, and more universal to leave it at this: everyone has some ideas about what we should do, with our inner life, with other people or the world, and this can applied. Whatever you think negativity or insanity is, you can use this practice of habits to work on that.

In one of my classes, I described this as a matter of speeding up problem solving. Everyone encounters repeating, problematic situations. Here's one: an argument you have with someone over and over, with no clear resolution. For me, I had that kind of argument with my wife, in the mornings, about my driving (which is not stellar, my driving that is, but still). I tried this technique, and not immediately, but after a little while, I found a solution. I got tired of having the same tension and arguing at that one time, I resolved not to be drawn into it, and quickly enough, found a solution. I'm not saying that our relationship is free from argument, whose is? But that problem was solved. (Incidentally, she drives most mornings now. This works for us.) A first step was seeing that a pattern had formed, arguing, and that I didn't want it to continue. (And, that for all the feeling and logic behind my words, during those arguments, they weren't working in that context.)

It doesn't always work. It did work, in that situation. Sometimes, as said earlier, you can fall from one habitual pattern into another. This can be surprising and unpleasant. With this, I think it's mostly a matter of degrees. If you're going to from one very entrenched, old habit, to another very old, entrenched habit, that's a problem. And sometimes, it just does happen. We're not talking about instant mastery, but a gradual, gentle process.

There should also be some feeling of freedom, or disorientation. If you're going through a well worn groove, it usually feels comfortable. You know the terrain, where to step.(Remember the Trungpa quote about the bad/good, good/bad memory, the enjoyment of one's own stench.) if you're going into unexplored territory, it feels, most of the time, freer, and a little disorienting, like switching hands when you're writing. I recommend applying the technique with a few things in your life. And see what happens, how it feels. Writing down how your work is going could be helpful. I have also included a few exercises I've come up with here in this book.

"Habit is a compromise effected between an individual and his environment."
Samuel Beckett

Selfless Self Help

Aikido

For some seven years or so, I did Tai Chi, diligently. I was no expert, over even seven intense years no one can become a master, although some proficiency is possible, depending on a number of factors, including, but not limited to, diligence. I did "the form," a set of solo, slow, fluid movements, every day, usually at night, if my memory is correct. Some days felt better than others, but overall, I made some progress. There was so much to pay attention to: posture, connecting various parts of the body, balance, an overall feeling of flow, even fighting applications.

I dropped out of college for about a year and a half, and took up the practice around that time. My dropping out had a lot to do with overusing drugs, and a general emotional turmoil. I returned to school, and found that there was an Aikido club on campus. They wore strange, traditional looking garb, and when they moved, in practice, it seemed flowing, odd, sometimes beautiful, and there was some power to it. It was also quite distinct from Tai Chi. I signed up, and dove in. I would go to practice a few nights a week, most weeks. There were certain instructors I liked more than

others, and I would look forward to their classes. Many classes
were taught by college students.

One thing, one really important thing for me, then, was that Aikido
gave me a community to hang out with. This was before I'd gotten
the courage up to sit and meditate with groups. I would, around
this time, do it on my own, but it took some courage for me to be
willing to sit with others. It made me uncomfortable. So did
Aikido, but there was so many positives to it that I guess I pushed
past the nerves. One of those pluses was the community. The
people were largely friendly, open, and they would spend time with
each other outside of class too. Aikido is a martial art founded in
the 20th century, on ancient Japanese principles. There is a
noticeable emphasis, for many teachers, on peace, kindness,
friendliness, and working through conflict in nonaggressive or
noncompetitive ways. This style goes back to the founder, Morihei
Ueshiba, who had a lot of experience as a martial artist and fighter,
but then gained some spiritual insight, and changed his view of
life, valuing peace and harmony above pure martial effectiveness.
(Don't get me wrong, I'm not judging other martial arts, or saying
there's no need for people to learn to effectively defend
themselves. I'm just explaining the style of Aikido, and maybe why

Selfless Self Help

it appealed to me and tended to create a friendly atmosphere on campus, at Oberlin.)

I suppose my work ethic and feeling for practice grew with Aikido. I definitely enjoyed the solidity and support of knowing I had a community who would talk to me, be kind to me, and help me get my life together, at least in terms of providing positive examples and a positive worldview. I was inspired, too, seeing the experienced students and older teachers who had something. Their movements and power were beautiful, and they had some odd energy to them, something I was fascinated with. This fascination with energy went back to my time pursuing Chinese martial arts.

"That's not the way out."

It was my senior year, and I was training with the head of the Aikido program at Oberlin. He was teaching a group class, and, as teachers would, he was circulating from partner group to partner group, demonstrating technique. He was leading me through something called "shiho nage," which involves the attacker's arm and shoulder being turned, sometimes painfully, up and out. In Aikido, there is much variety in terms of styles and approaches, but students are frequently taught to resist each other, to help create real, as opposed to showy or fake, techniques. I was resisting my teacher, trying to see if I could get out of his shiho nage. Without completely damaging my arm, he applied some pressure to let me feel that the kind of resistance I was offering would not end well. But, of course, it wasn't just about that.

Aikido is a world of metaphors. Language is something we'll look at more in-depth in the third section of this book. Metaphor and figurative language are almost universally used in mystical traditions as a teaching tool, and they are an extremely effective one. Many times, in class, our Aikido teachers would show something, turning to face the same way as the opponent, for instance, and talk about seeing things from another's perspective. We'd hear about not resisting the attacker, and this meant also not resisting life. "Moving off the line," was both an essential part of many techniques, which would usually end in a lock or throw, but also a way of looking at working skillfully with the energy of conflict as it arose in social situations.[13]

I trained and trained. I continued with the Tai Chi, although, at a certain point, my heart really was with the peaceful art of Aikido, the way of harmonizing energy, ki. I felt I was getting better, but then would fall flat. My pride would get larger, and then my teachers would deflate it, or show me some detail, large or small, I'd missed somehow. Eagerly, I waited for my teacher to call me up to the front of the class, to demonstrate something with him, and usually he wouldn't, unless, it seemed, I wasn't paying attention for a moment, and then he'd call my name. Once a class, more or less. I kept training for about a year or two after school ended, and it was invigorating, heartbreaking, mysterious. This was part of my education in warriorship, as Trungpa calls it, an experience of real community, sangha in Buddhist terminology, and something that certainly contributed to my meditation ability in many ways. I shouldn't leave out that physicality in training has been, continues to be, a big part of my studies, and Aikido both helped support that in pragmatic ways, but also in esoteric ways: I saw, in glimpses, that the body truly was a vehicle for otherworldly experience, but there was also no need to risk the trauma psychedelic trips could cause. It was a valid, and less dangerous path. You don't have to recover emotionally from a movement class the way you do from a strong trip.

So what is the way out? The way out is practice, a life of practice. In one of my more successful talks, at a library, I said this, point blank. It is about a lifelong commitment to practicing (something, which for me, means the Buddha dharma, but, for you, could be

something else). This is what I have termed a "meta-religious"
path. Find your way. The way is personal, specific, but traditional.
Selfless Self Help is about helping you with some basics, like in a
martial arts class, where you can sharpen the edge of those
essential basics, and then, from there, where you take it is a choice.

Selfless Self Help

Some Exercises

I prefer to teach these exercises in a class setting, just like the meditation practices, but the writing/thinking exercises can be done, with some efficacy, solo, unlike the meditation techniques (which have to be learned in person). First, informally, it's good to think about recurring problems in your life. Some of these may truly be caused by an other, as in the case of an abusive spouse, or living in a violent place, but some are probably related to your habits, especially your habitual ways of reacting. This can happen in small, or short term ways, as well as large, or long-term ways. Right now, I am working to get my career on track. My work life has been a mess, basically, since I started working near the end of high school. I haven't found that dream job, or been able to carve out a clear niche for myself, and haven't stayed on the same job for more than two and a half years. So, right now, personally, that's one pattern I'm working on changing: specifically by going back to school to get an M.A., but also just keeping in mind that I don't want to switch jobs too rashly, because I'm not happy with how that has worked out in the past. My career woes are an example of a really long term habit, or a set of habits manifesting over a long time.

114

You can see that part of this practice is extremely simple and hardheaded; see a pattern and decide to do something else, instead of repeating it for a lifetime. I don't want the long term pattern of changing jobs every few years, and moving every few years, too, to continue on, so I'm changing it. It can be interesting to look at long term patterns like these, and sometimes surprising (because it is easy, I find, to think you're being natural or just doing what you think is best, when actually, you're going along with some predetermined pattern). Generally, I think shorter term, smaller patterns, are easier to think of, when you start. So that's the first thing, just start thinking about patterns in your life, especially ones you are not happy with.

If you want, you can write some of those down, although I like to just think about them. See what feels right, and what works for you. The second is to go through the exercises I will list, and look at what they show. They might reveal some insights, or the informal reflection process might prove to be more valuable. The third thing, and the most important, is to work diligently to untie those habits as they appear in your life. This is supported by having a practice, and is done by choosing other, nonhabitual options. I will return to this point soon.

115

Have a look at this list. Write down, or think about the answers.

Time

Space

Knowledge

First, think about positive habits for each category. What are some good things you do relating in some ways to time, space, and knowledge?

Then, think about negative things. What are some negative things relating in some way to time, space, and knowledge?

Where do you want more of these three in your life? Less?

We have left off neutral habits, so if you want, you can devote some attention to neutral habits of these three, or things that don't fit clearly into one of the categories of good or bad.

Take some time to think about these things. It may be uncomfortable. I've had trouble getting myself to do this, so I understand that it can be uncomfortable. Resistance may come up. I think that sensation is, in this case, a good indicator, too, that there is something to look at. Once you've gone through the exercises, resolve to start implementing the solution, to find other choices. This could mean planning your actions, being in the moment, but will probably be some combination of both. Some of your answers will probably highlight important issues, and some will be less significant. This is fine. Some of the answers are not as charged, like the food and entertainment questions. Just remember that we are ripping through the cocoon, so, over time, any habitual areas should begin to open up. Your whole life is involved in the process of waking up. It is a lifelong commitment, and one that involves all aspects of life. The final question is larger, and does not need addressing in the same way the others do. Just think about it, and what it means. The last question is about observing and understanding, rather than changing or implementing new choices.

I found that it was uncomfortable mostly because of my negative self images, and some issues that were barely below the surface, issues that I was half aware of. The negative self images were the hardest to deal with, but also a bit of a relief, like getting them down on paper got something moving.

Real fearlessness is the product of tenderness. It comes from letting the world tickle your heart, your raw and beautiful heart.

Selfless Self Help

You are willing to open up, without resistance or shyness, and face the world. You are willing to share your heart with others.
Chogyam Trungpa

Goals

I am not a very goal oriented person. I do think about goals in terms of practice however. The main goal of the practice of trying different options and retraining habits is spontaneity. We started off by looking at cocoon, a realm of safety, comfort, and the antithesis of a full life. We looked at TSK's version of this, with some talk about tension, constriction, and the self. Finally, Pema Chodron offered the simple yet powerful suggestion that we try something else. It is possible to become less robotic, or reactive, and more spontaneous. Everyone has some idea about how they want to be in the world, and there's always some gap between the reality of people, with their history, neurotic and delusional problems, and cultural indoctrination, and their ideals. History has shown that realization, reaching a version of human being that is marvelously free and empowered, is within reach. It has been done. It will be done again.

When I dropped out of school, I was about twenty, and I went to stay with my parents, as a lot of people do when they drop out. It was a tense time in our house, but I think it was probably the best thing for me at the time. I found work, got my own place, in the upper floor of a "historic house" where I was nominally the caretaker, and about a year and a half later, returned to school. Leaving school was an admission, for me, that my drug use had gone too far. I was unhappy just from not having the kind of friends I wanted, not liking the school I was enrolled in, many reasons, but drugs had made everything much harder. So, dropping out allowed me to admit defeat, in a way, and regroup. I found myself having what might have been panic attacks. I was panicking on a regular basis, at least. Walking down the street made me very anxious a lot of the time, and I would sometimes get very sweaty. This sounds a little ridiculous, but it was not fun at the time. I felt equally uncomfortable and confused in social situations. Cannabis made me feel paranoid, and the LSD and mushrooms I took also made my mind chaotic. I saw swirling patterns much of the time, especially in things like carpets and wood grain (not just when I was high, but all the time). The anxiety and depression, the difficulty socializing with people that had developed in previous years became stronger, up to the point at which I got clean, and this was actually a gradual process. It wasn't just like I decided to get my shit together, and the next day I was working, smiling widely, and free of substances. It took years to cut drugs out of my life, the ones I found harmful at least, not so much caffeine, and in some ways, it is something ongoing, to this day. I am not so tempted to call a drug dealer and try to get something these days, but it is not an impossibility, and knowing that means that my discipline keeps going. This speaks to the idea of good habits. From eating worse than I do today, to drinking and smoking things that made me a person I didn't like, I have built up good habits over the years. I would not start binge drinking again just to do something new. I wouldn't eat pasta and cheese a lot just to get away from the habit of eating a good deal of veggies. That kind of spontaneity wouldn't really be spontaneous.

As far as good habits, like these, on the level of caring for oneself and being healthy, reaching a basic level of health is probably good (so, not worrying too much about eating health food all the time, or being some kind of perfect health god). Then, there is room to mix things up and add variety within the good habits. If I see myself eating the same kind of curries every day for lunch, it's good sometimes to try some stir fries, or something new. This is fun. There are so many new foods and dishes to try. It might seem insignificant, but this journey is so much a matter of dissolving old ways of being. These old ways, inflexible ways, manifest in every part of our lives, so making even small changes in many areas can have a real impact. We can always change things up, while staying healthy, in a relaxed way. Doing drugs is a problematic and complex issue, one I won't address with much depth in this book, aside from how it has been part of my own growing up process.

I can't say that I didn't learn or see things, on those drugs. I'm not making an argument one way or the other about legalization, decriminalization, or the possibilities of psychedelics for expanding the mind. That's a different story, and one that's not really in the area this book covers. What I am saying is that I took it too far, and, as a result, my mind and body suffered greatly. Some people are smart enough to use moderation. That's something I'm just starting to learn, and not something that comes naturally to me. I tend to do everything obsessively, from playing guitar to writing to smoking weed.

I also had physical trouble walking and being balanced. This probably started around the time I was growing as a teenager, but became very pronounced after my time in college. I'm past thirty now, and just getting to the point where I have a good sense of balance (physical and mental), and can feel okay just walking down the street.

Karlins

Those years were hellish. I became trapped in my own craziness, and without meditation and a spiritual path I would have stayed lost. It wasn't that I had no good ideas, at the time, when I was on or recovering from drugs, but I needed a nondualistic practice (meditation) and a tradition within which to explore my own mind, and get some perspective. Having good ideas is never enough.

I can say safely now that I've gotten past the most difficult part. My life now isn't easy at all, but the extra challenges are gone. The feeling of chaos, wild emotions, panic, being lost in a maze of distorted thoughts, have a body that felt like it was turning against me, those are gone. I owe a debt of gratitude to many people, including my family, who supported me, even if they didn't know all the gory details, and the meditation teachers who have guided me.

When I was using drugs, I wasn't the kind of guy who preferred to get fucked up, rowdy, and go wild. I would withdraw into myself, even if I was in a crowd. I would get quiet, and shut down, kind of frozen within myself. This could make other people nervous, and so I soon enough started to avoid others, and just keep to myself. I would stay in my room as much as possible. My life oftentimes centered around getting drugs and taking them on my own. It was funny, because it took years of agonized sitting, unable to reach out or talk, feeling paranoid, before I could admit that I was not happy, and had to change something. Anyway, I withdrew, and focused on getting high. This was a drug induced cocoon. As many recovering addicts will tell you, drug abuse is a way of avoiding things you don't like and avoiding facing certain issues. I did not want to face the difficulties of socializing and being out in the world. The anger, fear, self doubt, and so on, that I grappled with post-drug use are another story entirely. My point is that I was avoiding dealing with these things. One strange nuance of this craziness is that addicts bring up and relish, in a way, the problems that they create and suffer from, like being unable to reach out or connect fully, in order to avoid other, deeper issues. There is a sad, rocky drama to creating one set of problems while ignoring, and avoiding another.

It was the right decision to clean up my act, and I felt a great relief when I knew that this was what I wanted to do, that there was no other way for me. The thing was, I still had to deal with how habitual I was. One layer of habits had been cleared away, the drugs, but many other layers were still there, and underneath all of that, a general style of uptightness and habituation.

I don't think I will ever be the most charming or outgoing guy. I believe everyone has a natural style which is incredibly difficult to change, and not a natural thing to change, at a fundamental level.[14] Some people are fundamentally sociable, or artistic, or great at organizing things. I'm naturally creative, and thoughtful, but not naturally a big people person. Whatever your style, progress can be made, and I am proof of this fact. I have never been healthier, saner, or felt more grounded. Some of this has to do with becoming more spontaneous. But, please remember this point: self improvement is good, that some thing, but to think that you will be able to completely overhaul yourself, or turn yourself into some sort of dream self, would be a recipe for disappointment and frustration. Getting out of the comfort zone of the cocoon is very healthy, but it is not equivalent to becoming an entirely different person.

We seek comfort, but we also need to live. How exactly that living manifests has a lot to do with the choices you make, how you work with your habits, and whether you develop a personal practice.

As human beings, we are basically awake and we can understand reality. We are not enslaved to our lives; we are free. Being free, in this case, means simply that we have a body and a mind, and we

Selfless Self Help

can uplift ourselves in order to work with reality in a dignified and

humorous way. If we begin to perk up, we will find that the whole

universe- including the seasons, the snowfall, the ice and the mud-

is also powerfully working with us. Life is a humorous situation,

but it is not mocking us. We find that, after all, we can handle our

world; we can handle our universe properly and fully in an uplifted

fashion.

The discovery of basic goodness is not a religious experience,
particularly. Rather it is the realization that we can directly
experience and work with reality, the real world that we are in.
Experiencing the basic goodness of our lives makes us feel that we
are intelligent and decent people and that the world is not a threat."
(Trungpa 16)

Part two

Compassion

What to Do

Any time you turn on the news, or see news online, you don't to
wait very long before you hear about people doing terrible things.
Sometimes it's celebrities doing terrible things, and then I think,
why can't they just be happy with their amazing wealth, and easy
lifestyle? Why can't people who have it so easy just be happy, and
live good lives? Sometimes it's ordinary people doing terrible
things. I wonder what I can do, worry and feel guilty. Oftentimes, I
just tune it out, uncaring.[15]

There is a lot you can do, and one thing is to develop compassion.
Before this, working on the habitual part of the mind, and building
a daily meditation practice are things we talked about, and these
are good, helpful. Once you have those things going, compassion
is next.

Selfless Self Help

As people who aspire to live meaningful lives, you have ideas about how other people should act, the way others should behave and make choices. I was just with a friend who is really talkative. He doesn't like silence, it seems. I understand this, silence is difficult. I had some good times talking with him, and enjoyed the company, but I also judged him, a little, for being so talkative. Maybe this is my Buddhist training; we are told not to engage in "idle chatter" just to cover up silence. Anyway, I judged him for it. Whenever you have ideas about other people's actions, or even attitudes, you are one tiny step away from judgment.

It's not that judgment is terrible. It doesn't make you a mean person to judge. Everyone does it. It does mean that you're distancing yourself from a certain kind of reality, what I like to call "mirroring." Judgement, hypocrisy, and compassion all go together in Selfless Self Help. Compassion, as it is defined in this system, is slightly different from how people ordinarily think of it. In Selfless Self Help, I say "hypocrisy is compassion." When I looked down on my friend for being talkative and being nervous about silence, I was being a hypocrite. As I mentioned, I have some understanding of this; silence is difficult. My understanding comes from my personal experiences with silence in my own life. Actually, silence itself has been a huge theme in my life. I remember the tense silences around the dinner table when I was a kid. I've always fled from silence when I've been by myself. It can make me sad and nervous. When I was older, high school and college, I didn't know what to say when groups of people "hung out" sometimes, and felt alternating pulls toward speaking, just to not create an awkward moment, and toward not speaking, for some reason, maybe to get people to talk to me individually. Over the years, I've very slowly become more comfortable with the silence, and this feels intuitively very correct.

My hypocrisy, sitting in the truck with my friend, was to see him as someone who's bad with pauses in conversation, when I am too, still uncomfortable with it, even if, for me, it's less. When I can catch these moments of hypocrisy, I can develop some compassion. In fact, moments of hypocrisy are compassion shining through, like the brilliance of a smile illuminating someone's face.

You should examine yourself and ask how many times you have tried to connect with your heart, fully and truly. How often have you turned away, because you feared you might discover something terrible about yourself? How often have you been willing to look at your face in the mirror, without being embarrassed? How many times have you tried to shield yourself by reading the newspaper, watching television, or just spacing out? This is the sixty-four thousand dollar question: how much have you connected with yourself at all in your whole life? (Trungpa 30-1)

Connecting with yourself, being with yourself, not turning away, might seem to be individual practices, but they can't be said to be either individual or other-related practices. When you start to connect with yourself, and stop running so much, your relations with others will tend to change. In the first section, when we talked about habits, the focus was more individual: seeing ones own pain and cocoon, seeing how we feel trapped or constricted. Here, with compassion, the emphasis is not totally off one's individual experience, that's still there, but there's much more attention paid to others, specifically how others mirror us, and vice versa.

This mirroring, which somehow happens in many ways, sometimes surprising ways, begins to point in the direction of a sacred life, our own. It is one thing to say that life is inherently sacred, or that you believe life is more than just materialistic or rational concerns, but another to experience this on a daily basis. The experiential path of the sacred is the direction we're headed in, and it can be found in such mundane interactions as conflict with neighbors, stress generated by commuting, office hardships. Any time you judge, you become a hypocrite, and anytime you are a hypocrite, your compassion is bursting forth, albeit in a surreptitious way.

Compassion is like the tree that continually pushes its roots through the ground, not caring for an instant that the sidewalk is made of concrete, the sidewalk it crushes and destroys over and over.

Not Convinced

The whole of creation in time and space may participate in a most remarkable intimacy, with wisdom, compassion, and moral conduct of the highest order it's spontaneous expression. Tarthang Tulku, Love of Knowledge, 93

One reasonable logical objection to the hypocrisy/compassion idea is that, well sometimes, we do pick out other people's flaws or mistakes, but this is not always how it works. Let me try to give two examples. Earlier, I mentioned the talkative friend, and how I understood that situation. (Of course, there are other ways to understand such a situation, and many alternative understandings could be helpful, creative, interesting, but for now, I'm sticking with the topic at hand.) I said that I judged him in spite of my own difficulties with silence, or maybe somehow because of this personal struggle. At the same time, I said that I felt I'd come a long way in this regard; this is true. I am so much more comfortable with silence now than I was as a young man, and I'm happy with this development. So, you could ask, is the hypocrisy there real? Isn't it simplistic or off the mark to say that my judgment mirrored my issue? In some cases, this is true.

Here is what to do when that happens. First, know the instance as an example of "still a long way to go." I'm making progress, but I still have a long way to go. Seeing my own problems in others doesn't mean that those problems, whether they happen to be anger, or cowardice, or being unable to handle pauses, it doesn't mean that they are problems that have never been addressed, or that no progress has been made. It means that more progress could be made.

So the first thing is still a long way to go. The second thing is that, yes, indeed, sometimes when you look for hypocrisy mirroring, you may not find anything. Here are actually two parts to this second part.

1. Still a long way
2. Yes indeed
3. Use the medicine of gentleness
4. Generalize and look again

Using the medicine of gentleness means that, by using others as a way of cutting through our own neurosis, we can ofttimes be too harsh, too hard on ourselves. Pema Chodron is famous for talking extensively about this. "The most difficult times for many of us," she writes in her book *When Things Fall Apart*, "are those we give ourselves."

Seeng our own issues in our judgements naturally will become a form of self denigration. I can pretty much guarantee that this will happen as a kind of toxic byproduct of trying to use the technique. The good news there is that, with any meditation technique, whether "on or off the cushion," done formally or informally, there will tend to be these toxic byproducts, and that is just part of the process. I suggest that you notice it, and try to let it go. Don't buy into it. It could be useful to notice when, and how much it's happening; probably when this harshness occurs, it will occur when you're generally having a hard time or feeling stressed out.

Just as there was a Trungpa quote earlier about basic goodness, and he talked about feeling like you're intelligent and decent, and that the world is not inherently threatening, Pema has written many times about this same thing: the experience of life as either one of self respect and experiencing our world, or self hatred, and fearing life. Being gentle with yourself is usually the cure for the latter problem, and seeing how judgmental you are must be sweetened with gentleness. (Or it will backfire, and you'll give up.)

Generalizing and looking again means that if I see some problem in someone else's actions, and don't see it as a reflection of my own, I could generalize and perhaps find something to work on. Let me mention another example. It bothers me when other drivers tailgate. It feels aggressive, and I can get upset, glancing obsessively in my rear view mirror, until we part ways. Now, I don't tailgate much. I used to, but my driving has gotten saner over the years. If I judge someone for tailgating me, that doesn't mean that I need to stop doing that exact thing. Generalizing, maybe I could still be a less aggressive driver in other ways. Maybe I could be less aggressive, in other parts of my life. Maybe I could be less like a tailgater in conversation, and stop interrupting.

It's easy to see how this could go too far. When you generalize in this way, it can become an exercise in absurdity. Seeing the tailgater as a reminder to be less aggressive is probably too much. Not that I'm totally without aggression, just that it seems like a stretch to me (and this is a very key point- you will know, on some level, when your hypocrisy is really on point, or when you're trying too hard and it's a stretch, usually some slight feeling of embarrassment will happen when it is accurate). When you generalize, roll the ideas over in your mind, allowing that maybe you are being a hypocrite, or maybe not. Maybe, in this instance,

135

you're just being too hard on yourself, and taking the instruction a little too far. Another way this could go too far is if one were to make everything obsessively about oneself. Suddenly, everything is a message, a teaching, and it's all about us, and how to improve. This technique, the judgment technique, will naturally tend to cloud our unencumbered communications and experiences of others. When this happens, try to bring yourself back to some kind of presence. When your mind gets too discursive and self-involved, bring yourself back.

Now, I should mention, that even if there is no self denigration happening, and you see that your judgement is not some sort of reflection or hypocrisy, it could just be something unrelated to you. This does occasionally happen. You see someone doing something you dislike, and when you look inside, you can tell it is not your problem. If I were to see people brawling in the street, and find it disgusting, that wouldn't reflect on me. I'm not someone who does this.

The first and third points, still a long way to go, and generalizing, may seem the same. The difference is that, with the first, it means that you've caught yourself being a hypocrite in an area you've done some work in, made some progress in, but could still go farther with. If I see someone being impatient, it doesn't mean that I'm a terribly impatient wreck, it could mean that I've become more patient over time, but could still get even patient. The third is more about taking the focus off of a specific mistake someone/we makes, seeing it as part of a larger issue, and working on that.

The quote from Tarthang at the start of the chapter was less about neurosis, and more about some kind of mysterious, mystical level of reality. The two must go hand in hand. By working on our limitations, which is a kind of purification, it becomes more and more possible to get in touch with sacredness. In my difficulties and mistakes in the drug realm, this was most definitely something I was looking for, an experience of real, palpable sacredness. I am sure many folks come to drug abuse because of this longing. The path of a meditator, as I see it, is about doing the work yourself, with a clear head, to encounter the sacred. Others may find it works to include drugs in their path, which means both that I disagree with some, who are misguided, wasting valuable years in dreamland, and some others just have a different approach from me. At first, it may seem like the common sense, gritty work of purifying interactions with the other, or others, is distinct from God, the holy, the transcendent, whatever label you like, but they are, as my teacher likes to say, "nonseparate." The strange

Selfless Self Help

goodness of sacred world is hidden below the surface of emotion interaction, and I have no idea why this is.

Keep Working

Although we've gone through the section of the book where habits were the point of focus, the work of seeing them, and trying out new ideas, in the hope of manifesting spontaneity, never ends. It could only end when you've become totally free, and spontaneous, which is to say, realized. That does happen. History is full of stories of great masters, Christian, Sufi, Jewish, whatever. But it's not easy, and for most of us, just getting a little closer to that level will have to suffice, at least in this lifetime. Therefore, working on unknotting one's habits is a lifelong practice. A Tony Robbins quote comes to mind, about how flies stuck in a bottle struggle to get out again and again, and how most people live lives like this.

You can do what you find meaningful with your life. You can live in ways that are satisfying. You do not need to give in to a constant flow of habitual negativity. If this sounds like some sort of infomercial or meme or like something people tell themselves just to build themselves up artificially, okay. Be skeptical. I would never expect someone to dive into any training without a grain of salt. Then again, at what point does skepticism become an excuse for holding back, avoiding living new experiences, or facing one's problems? At what point do the seemingly logical, reasonable objections begin to reek of nervousness?

I have applied the training on habitual patterns in my life, and I'm glad that I did. It is usually extremely hard. I did theatre in high school, but only because everyone had to as part our schooling, and I wasn't the type to just skip class or say no. However, I found it unbearable. I hated being on the spot in front of teachers and classmates, and the moments of being in front of an actual audience were nightmares of burning lights, shaking nerves, and intense presence. My point is that I'm not the natural improviser, on that level. So, quite possibly, I won't be the most outrageously spontaneous guy, even years from now. You never know, but I do feel that people's personalities are not entirely fluid. This being said, I have gotten better at being able to improvise, and even find my way out of emotional and communicative ruts. I have applied this training to my life, and found it useful, challenging, and sometimes mysterious. In a way, the entire universe is made out of interlocking patterns. This means that, although work in this area can be very down to earth and practical, it can also be mysterious and mystical.

Along with the pattern practices, and compassion practice (recently introduced), there is meditation practice. I hope that you've been doing this regularly, at least once a day for a few minutes. If you find it more beneficial, something such as prayer, yoga, et cetera, is fine. I do recommend finding one thing and sticking with it for a time (as opposed to trying on a new practice every day). At this point in my class, when I have taught this material in a classroom setting, I like to introduce two new meditation techniques. I won't go into those much here. This is because I can't teach them through a book, and to try would suggest that I can, and encourage readers to do the practices without in person instruction. It is not essential that you learn the specific practices I mention in this book, but it is important that you get one on one instruction if you're learning a new practice, at least once or twice. Advice on finding a reasonable, ethical, decent meditation teacher can be found easily. I have found that, right now at least, there seems to be a fair amount of anxiety around the creepy spiritual leader. There are, of course, teachers out there who want to take a lot of your money, or manipulate you, or have sex with you. I did not encounter this much at all, but it does happen (and I'm a guy, so that may be a factor). If you're concerned about that, when looking for a meditation teacher, there are many things you can do.

Selfless Self Help

Don't make serious commitments right away, before you know a group and what they're about. Do some research online, knowing full-well that the Internet is not always correct. Don't assume you have to pay a lot for teachings, or, conversely, that all teachings must be free. Distinguish between your intuition and your biases. You can usually find group meditation sessions, where they'll offer instruction, so if that makes you more comfortable, or seems safer, you can try that.

The technique I introduced before was the body scan. The techniques for this part are mindfulness, and contemplation (which uses mindfulness as its foundation). I think one strong point of contemplative meditation is that it can be used by anyone, of any faith, to contemplate whatever religious text they find powerful. It is also good because it shows that thinking can become a part of meditation. Contrary to popular belief, thoughts are not bad, and not something meditation seeks to destroy.

By looking gently at patterns, turning hypocrisy into compassion, and having a daily practice of some kind of another, we are slowly but surely dissolving the film that has obscured the beauty of reality. This beauty is not religious, and it is not opposed to religion either. When I've heard teachers say that this experience is "your birthright," it has seemed a little archaic (even if now I am starting to understand that). If birthright sounds archaic, think of it as the self wanting to say hello to us, not the individual self, but the larger self out there. Or, if that, again, seems weird, think of it as a clarification process. We're clearing our heads. Whatever beauty or energy or goodness we find along the way becomes less and less arguable. Once you experience, no one can tell you otherwise.

How Does it Feel?

The bad news is you're falling through the air, nothing to hang on to, no parachute. The good news is there's no ground. Trungpa

This experience is what he often referred to as "groundlessness," which is related to, but not the same as what is called "emptiness" by Buddhists. Groundlessness is, in a way, happening all the time. It's most noticeable when there are moments of change, surprise, new things coming into view, or old things going away. Any notion of freedom or realization has to take into account this experience of no ground; there are different versions of how to do it, but it has to be addressed somehow, mostly because it's such a big part of life, and the pain of life.

When you do the compassion practice I outlined, groundlessness is the one of the things you will likely feel. There is a moment of feeling justified in disliking something or someone, a moment of questioning and seeing hypocrisy, and then a moment of groundlessness. It's like the instance in an argument when you go from feeling totally in the right, to having a glimpse of the insight that there might be another side, and you might actually be wrong.

Karlins

(This latter example could be from Pema. It feels like something she might say, so if I stole that, I apologize.)

When practicing the compassion technique, groundlessness gets introduced. This happens in the moment, but has larger implications. I don't think I need to explain those quite yet, and I'm sure you can imagine what they might be. Sitting meditation is also training in groundlessness, so these two things can feedback into each other, compassion and meditation. Over time, this is a practice can make you a little more open, more able to understand others, and more flexible.

Among the indications that a vision born of new knowledge is in operation is a tolerance for ourselves and others, born of the global perspective that comes with a more comprehensive knowing. (Tarthang Tulku, Love of Knowledge 91)

Equality and hierarchy are very subtle and difficult to measure out. One part of what is happening with this compassion meditation is a reminder of equality. We're all human. We all have troubled minds, difficulties, and positive qualities too. Equality is the opposite of the feeling that you are a bystander, someone totally unique, separate from the rest of humanity, struggling to win against the rest of humanity. There are many struggles in life, even an easy one like mine, but this idea of being at odds with, and even victimized by the world, by humanity, is neither totally accurate or very useful, and both are considerations. So, when you recognize that you're pointing a finger at someone else's blind spot, which turns out to be your own blind spot, equality is, for a second, realized. It's a little bit like being in a movie where the camera is shooting from the perspective of one guy, and then it goes to a far away shot of a crowd, or a building. This must lead to tolerance, this new vision, and new knowledge. Some of this tolerance happens pretty seamlessly and naturally, some of it has to be self-enforced (ie, there's an element of discipline to it). I mentioned hierarchy and equality in the same breath, so I should say something about hierarchy. Seeing shared humanity means that we are not blameless, a victim, or perfect. At the same moment, this doesn't mean that everyone is at the same place, in any aspect of life. Shared humanity means kindness and compassion are possible, and people's differences mean that their roles need to be based on strengths, and how they fit together.

Everyone has their own natural strengths and weaknesses. I've gotten less physically clumsy over the last few years (remember, this goes back to the mind/body chaos I experienced on drugs, and coming off of them).[16] This, the diminishment of my clumsiness,

146

has something to do with physical training, and also working menial jobs, like being a baker, and a housecleaner. Being graceful and coordinated has not been my natural strength for some time, although I've definitely worked on it, and I'd suggest that any meditator could benefit a lot from working on this. This is part of what Trungpa called "synchronizing mind and body," and what his students later amended to call "synchronizing body, speech, and mind." With regards to hierarchy, I would not make he best soccer coach. I'm not great at soccer, and I don't know much about it. For me to be the boss or manager of many soccer coaches or players would be even more odd. That's hierarchy. All of us, soccer players and otherwise, share a humanity, a heart, and yet we also are quite varied.

Here is a quote from Trungpa, on the topic of what he called "drala," the choice of which term was revolutionary in its own way. Drala has a lot to do with perceptions as gates to the divine, perceptions as magical and sacred and beautiful. I am including it because this transcendent side of things will become more relevant in the next section (soon) and because the idea of many-ness and oneness working together comes up.

Selfless Self Help

Discovering drala... to see with the heart, so that what ins invisible to the eye becomes visible as the living magic of reality. There may be thousands or billions of perceptions, but they are still one. If you see one candle, you know exactly what all the candles in the world look like. They are all made out of fire, flame. Seeing one drop of water can be seeing all water.

The new vision, and new knowledge Tarthang mentioned have a lot to do with diving into our shared humanity, which is groundless. It is both surprising in the way groundlessness, and has a grounding quality to it. When you see it, it can bring you back to yourself in the moment. Just like the fire and water mentioned above, people are equal, and also individual.

It's Been a Journey of Sorts Already

I have said a bit about my work to get off drugs, and get my life together. This book isn't tell-all, and I haven't bored you with the complete horror of what neuroses and idiocies I trudged through, over those years. During that time, I also started dating, kissed a girl for the first time (in college, so, you can see that I was very shy in many regards) and started learning about that part of life, love. Of course, a lot of people are slow starters when it comes to sex and love and dating, and a lot of people grow up some in college. This is a time of maturing, more for some than others. I worked during my time as a student, too, not a lot, but consistently, and mostly as a dishwasher or server at the cafeterias. (I still remember one time that I took mushrooms while working as a pizza server/reheated at a big cafeteria, misjudged when they'd kick in, and had to work while everything got weird and fluid.) I am mentioning this because work has taught me as much as dating and being married have.

I think the path is both pragmatic and unpragmatic, and I think it is about maturing. The latter term is worth remembering. It is decidedly not exciting or magical. Meditation has to make you a better person, a better significant other, a better worker. But maybe those categories are distracting, meditation needs to churn out more mature people. This is very commons sense, and a good guideline. Later, I'll talk about eccentricity, so I don't mean maturity as some kind of conformity, but as being a stable, kind, disciplined person. Imagine going to a talk with a priest or meditation teacher or yogi, and seeing them say something needlessly cruel, or get annoyed at someone for a tiny slight. It is not common, in my experience, but I have seen teachers be immature, and it is embarrassing, and takes away from the power of a good class. The bigger problem is that moments like those indicate that the teacher in question is immature, and thus, maybe not ready to lead.

This has been a huge part of my own practice over the last couple of years, trying to teach meditation. I set out to do this about two or three years ago, and there have been some good classes, and some bad ones (along with quite a few where nobody showed up). I have been so nervous teaching that I have talked too fast, been unable to organize thoughts clearly. I have had students who annoyed me, with whom I had an unpleasant dynamic, over a few classes, and this did not help the feel or experience of those sessions. I have lost my train of thought millions of times. I have seen my pride and arrogance puff up when answering questions, or seeing that a class is going decently. All of these have been learning experiences, and it is my job, now, to remember these lessons, and work consistently on them.

Over time, my teaching has gotten a little better, and more consistent. The main thing I have been trying to learn, as I teach, is how to become more mature. I see so many of my faults in the classroom, and I want to be a good teacher. A good teacher, in the meditation context, has to be a mature person. Otherwise, what is their authority? Why listen to them at all? At times when I've been tempted to do stupid things, like honking too much, in traffic, or being rude to people, or not getting along with my family, this has been in the back of my mind. I have taught a number of classes, in many different places, and I guess you could say I'm a meditation teacher, now, but I still feel like I'm earning it, making it real. Being a mature adult is the most important part of this. (Learning how to practice a meditation technique is, by comparison, pretty easy and straightforward.)

But what of being pragmatic and unpragmatic? The becoming a better guy or girl part is pragmatic (as is working on your habits

Selfless Self Help

and solving problems). The road never ends there, however, and this is one major place where Selfless Self Help differs from other approaches. Becoming decent, and seeing the sacred world are both invaluable.

Perhaps the best way to stimulate knowledge... is just to acknowledge what we do not know. A healthy regard for not-knowing marks the emergence of knowledge in the midst of the unknown. Learning to recognize the signs that we do not know that we do not know, we know where to direct our inquiry so that knowledge can emerge. (Tarthang Tulku LON)

This openness, to admit we don't know, is beautiful. It is both a moment in which new solutions, ideas, and possibilities can be reached, and a good moment, an end, in itself. To merely emphasize that openness helps solve problems is crass, a form of materialism. You see this, I think, with some modern popular forms of mindfulness meditation, where it is sold as a way to make things better or easier, when this is not the only goal. You have to see that problem solving is excellent, but never enough. The beauty and dignity of not knowing, of a moment of being, must be appreciated, acknowledged, respected. This is its own fruition, like a flower growing from space itself.

152

Karlins

Art

Studying or enjoying poetry and other written forms of art can be helpful. Just like it can be deadening to limit your language to a baseline of basic, robotic responses, it can be deadening to take in the same basic, robotic media. There's a lot to be learned from seeing how good writers use words. There's a lot to be learned about intuition there. On the whole, many, if not most, art seems to address spiritual concerns. That seems to be inescapable. Meaning is there.[17]

On top of that, art itself has a lot to teach about energy, spirit, and the sacred (which could also be called spookiness, I think, I was thinking about this today, of sacred world as a world inhabited in many angles, rife with beings, which gets spooky sometimes).

While the skillful use of language has a lot to teach about energy, so does all art. One angle of approach when it comes to energy is communication, the connection and interaction of things. Art is about communication. Magic is about communication. Art is magic. (Good art is good magic, bad art is still magic, just not very effective.)

154

Dimensions of space, dimensions of reality somehow contain things, and when magic occurs, when communication occurs, these dimensions can yield their bounty (not in terms of "manifesting" or getting rich, but in terms of feelings, sensations, perceptions). If this sounds very abstract and strange, just think about what happens when you watch a movie, and a certain atmosphere is created. You see a character enter the action, and you know, without much time having passed, what they are, what kind of person they are and what they're doing. Somehow, space has been filled, space has opened and various energies have crossed that gap. This has been done by the graceful mixing of colors, sounds, glimpses.

I grew up around art- large bookshelves full of works by poets, Jungian psychologists, books of paintings or cave paintings, art in frames on the walls, trips to museums on weekends. Music. I have always loved music, as I guess most people have, living in this time of free access and digitization, but I've always loved it, and my parents introduced me to it, in the form of LP's, and the radio. I remember that we had Philip Glass records, which I think I liked at an early age, oddly, *Einstein on the Beach, Akhenaten,* and some others I forget. There were kid's records, like *Free to Be You and*

Me, and Raffi, plastic binders of story tapes, like *Jacob Two Two and the Hooded Fang*. Lots of classical music, which could be on at odd times, but always, it seemed, for holidays, birthdays, et cetera, to create the right atmosphere. I had this little tape to help me go to sleep, which was a struggle for me for almost thirty years, my "sleep tape" as my parents called it. On it was, among some other beautiful songs, Pachelbell's *Canon*. I found it strangely beautiful, moving, sad. It made me cry, filled my heart with feelings that were powerful and incomprehensible and magnetic, and held a special place in my personal history. It disappeared from my life until I was in my twenties, and met my future wife, whose cell phone ringtone was the *Canon*. Of course, it was played at our wedding.

I tried to explain the meaning of this song to people, around this time, but somehow, couldn't quite communicate it, and this is often the way it seems to work with art, especially personally meaningful art. This is something- art is personally meaningful. This is where I see its power being. Yes, there is the historical side, which can be fascinating, and other ways of appreciating it or understanding it in various contexts, but for me, it's mostly about my experience being there, in a moment, however short or long, with the work of art. It could be a pop song. It could be a painting.

The point is that something emotional, energetic, and meaningful happens in that moment. It cannot be explained away, most times, by saying that it's merely personal, implying that it's some kind of preference (unless it's a fake reaction or an affectation of some kind, like proclaiming that you like something fashionable, maybe this is why "hipsters" are so unpopular right now, because they're notorious for a sense of affectation and self inflicted irony, which reminds us of our own occasional, more or less, affectations and less-than-sincere preferences). The next step, then, beyond that sacred moment of appreciation, is the stepping out of the museum moment, where everything seems to be art. If you've spent a little time in a museum, and then left, and somehow, without you knowing, your mind has changed slightly, and you're looking at the world like a painting or a sculpture, then you understand.

We will always come back to the start, with cocoon. I think this is how it works with basic teachings. One thing art does, by breaking up the ice floes inside of us, as Kafka thought of it, is bring people out of their self-sheltered, hardened existence. I have the feeling that, for most Westerners living above the poverty line, we are much less hardened than anyone else has been, in the past. Our lives can be stressful, but are pretty safe, pretty easy, historically speaking, and we are bathed in food and entertainment. Still, we harden ourselves and allow ourselves to be hardened by habit, by holding back, by anxiety, by negativity, and by avoiding the new and chaotic. Art has the power and grace to gently (usually) unzip this hard outer casing. Emotion flows. Tears may flow, or at least, appear for a second. We remember dreams, not in the sense of ambitions, or special plans, but just a sense of possibility and having dreams. The robotic responses, taking in the same media again and again, these can be connected. So art opens things up, like meditation, like the practice of trying something different in the moment.

Part of this seems to be that we need some training, however informal, in appreciation. I'm very lucky in that my family loves art, and taught this to me, the love of art, and the language of art. I'm lucky in that I've had some teachers who got art, and showed me how to get it, too, even if, at the time, I was 99% likely to be a jaded, resistant, know it all young person, a young person who usually wouldn't understand or take to heart their lessons until he was older. It's the stepping out of the museum experience, again. We need that. It's not as obvious as saying that the whole world is art, although it can be sometimes, and that's part of it, but it's that, as students, we need refreshers and reminders. We need transmission. There are a million ways to get this education, this refreshment, but without that, it's impossible to know how to attune your senses to an object, whether a song on the radio or a sculpture in a garden, and respond, and think and listen.

The responses, the thoughts, the listening, can be based on some historical or book knowledge, this artist did this, this style looks like that or a reaction to that, but a lot of it is personal, and intuitive. I hesitate to call it "intuitive" here, because the term suggests, I think, something a little more pragmatic or small than I'd like. With a little education, whether from books, the internet, radio, what have you, those internal conversations can become sharper, more alive. Of course, this should sound like meditation, and meditation connects well with this kind of thinking practice or appreciation practice. As we begin, more, to talk about the sacred, this kind of looking inward, working with intuition and inner senses, is key. Luckily, the training in loving art, and seeing art in life not only aids this, but is addictively enjoyable. We just need some guidance from other people, in some form, and reminders that the unthinking consumption of information sources is not the only way, or the best way to have fun.

Selfless Self Help

Capturing

Energy and space go together, just like words and silence. In meditation practice, people work with both energy and space. In fact, it is an extremely sophisticated way to work with those two things. It is sophisticated, I think, because it is so simple, and so counterintuitive. This happens in different ways, one of which is through following, or trying to follow, or resisting, the instructions. These instructions take the form of language.

When you do your job, go from place to place, try to accomplish things, try to work with the teachings on habituation and compassion, you can learn things. Then you go back to practicing, which is essential. That brings things down to earth. I find, and I don't think I'm the only one, that things very easily get intellectual and divorced from reality when I'm out there in the world. The main thing that grounds me and helps me process stuff is meditation.

When I feel myself getting too "in my head" or abstract, this is being spacey, and we all know the idioms that go along with this, spacing out, space cadets, head in the clouds. By seeing this, and doing something about it, such as a meditating, I am working with space, and I am bringing things to earth, coming back down to earth. When I was a kid, I used to like playing outside, at least sometimes, but hated gym class and sports. As I've gotten older, I've learned to enjoy and appreciate physical things, and one reason is the earthy quality they have to them. This earthiness is not something to scorn or laugh off. It's real, and, more importantly, it can be used as a tool. These things, like exercise, or cleaning, walking around, movement arts, are not usually as profound as meditation (unless they become meditation in and of themselves, which is a different story) but they are similar in some ways, and they are very useful.

Since earth has a function and is useful when it comes to relating to sky, can't the opposite be said? We're just barely scratching the surface, but I think so. One way this happens for me is in terms of silence. Silence and pausing are ways to inject space into a life, and it's usually very challenging for me. I want to do chores (maybe I want is not the right way to put it, but the thought arises), I want to watch movies, I want to go on the internet. But when I can effectively pause, and stop being afraid of being haunted by silence, my heart relaxes somewhat. Things look up.

Selfless Self Help

As you continue to practice, you can learn different ways to work with energy. Some are simpler than others. Then you can apply these things to your off the cushion life. One goal is recognize space as it happens, and energy as it happens. Then another is to invoke space, or invoke various energies in ways that are helpful to you, and to others. Through all of these things, the bottom line is that the self does not become more closed off, or built up. A meditator develops ways to use language, space, and energy, but this shouldn't mean that the meditator becomes arrogant, manipulative, or sealed off from the world. Energy leads to groundlessness, just like words. This can be

pleasant or unpleasant, this groundlessness. Becoming a more skillful meditator does not mean that you create a safer, easier world for yourself, and this self that you experience is how that happens; this self is naturally porous and punctured by interaction. Becoming a practitioner does not take away that porous, tender quality.

Something and Nothing in Concert

This brings me to a discussion of balancing. This term, balance, is one I'd resisted for many years. It smacked, to me, of the kind of New Age or yoga style that was flimsy, unrealistic, lacking in depth. Of course, often the things that we have as pet peeves or that we resist so much are often what we need, or need to learn from. I'm starting to appreciate the term balance, and the principle of balance. It is not coincidence that physical balance, which deteriorated when I was younger, around the time I got involved heavily in drugs, has started becoming better over the last few years (just as I began to appreciate the principle). My physical balance has improved a jot, and so has my general skill in balancing things in my life (work, fun, relationship, family, art). I continue to work on both. There does seem to be, for me at least, a correspondence.

I don't think I can overemphasize what this exemplifies. Maybe I already have. Words as metaphors tune you in to metaphoric reality. The way a therapist might pick up on certain metaphoric language you use unconsciously, you can too. (Which is not to say that you don't need a therapist, or that you do, just that this way of listening to things can be very powerful, and a key to sacred world.) When I began to find ways to balance myself in the midst of my life, in interactions with my world, so I was not as easily upset, my understanding of the word itself changed. Metaphors are doors to reality.

I worked on my physical balance, which really has to do with many interrelated skills, including moving balance and stationary balance, through my time as a Tai Chi person, and an Aikidoka. In Tai Chi, I worked at the form, in which you slowly shift your weight from one leg to another. Sometimes there are single leg balancing poses, with symbolic names, like Rooster Stands on One Leg, sometimes known as Golden Rooster Stands on One Leg. This training is very difficult sometimes, and I can remember my legs feeling like jelly, shaky, after I started doing form work. Aikido does not really have form work per se, but a firm stance is emphasized, and balance is trained through partner work, and learning to roll/take falls. Learning to do rolls and take falls when someone uses a technique was scary, but exhilarating and fun, eventually. During this time, however, even as I worked on my physical development and coordination, things went very slowly in other parts of my life. A greater degree of balance took many years to even begin taking root. Here, of course, I'm talking about finding a way to have a life that felt full, not too crazy, and not too focused on just one thing, and in a lot of ways, sending my way through this learning process was just a part of growing up: learning workplace skills, learning relationship skills, learning what I found satisfying and meaningful in my own spare time. That's just basic stuff everyone tends to learn around this time, around their college or post college years.

Many things happened between my years of drug abuse and agony, and my current state of being pretty much okay. I lived in a few different places, California, Massachusetts, Ohio, New York, eventually Thailand. I worked with a couple of meditation teachers, became a Buddhist (in my heart, at first, then officially, later, with a ceremony called taking refuge). I even found a teacher to work with, a main teacher. It was this process of working with teachers, particularly my main teacher, that led to my understanding of what balance means for me, and I suppose it had a range of meanings for every person. Through this teacher student relationship, finally, after years of struggle, I was able to see what I needed to do. I say this because years of training led me to where I am today, but it was finding a teacher that was the most important part. His words sparked something mysterious and powerful.

I wanted to talk about balance mostly because I wanted to talk about words. (I'll write more later about balance, physical balance, with regards to my psychedelic drug use, so, in a slightly separate context. I hope you don't mind the repetition too much.) The metaphor is the primary way words are used to transmit wisdom in the meditation tradition, and this can be seen in works of poetry, like Rumi, classic religious texts, like the Bible, but to experience it happening in the now, in a moment, as you sit across from an empowered teacher is something quite different. I have quite a few stories about these metaphorical teaching moments. One involves talking to a teacher, in New York, when he said that he thought I seemed very considerate, but also a "square peg in a round hole," which was true. I have contemplated that, and worked to negotiate that for years now, what it means to be like that, and how, if I want, to fix it. Another teacher told me that I was "taking very small steps," and I took this to mean that I should consider taking some leaps in my life. Soon after, I got engaged and moved overseas for about a year. This taught me so much.

So teachers will often use metaphors. They engage the student almost automatically, connecting in to some very old part of the language brain, some basic interpretive structure, really one of the most basic abstractions, if not the most basic. My point isn't that metaphors are a classic teaching device, my point is that the world itself seems to function in a metaphorical way. To put this in other terms, the way people are, and the way the world and people mesh, seems to be metaphorical. I don't look like a peg, but the instruction about taking bigger steps was based on the fact that the teacher had seen me during walking meditation. I was literally taking small steps, which goes back to my balance and physical issues. He knew, I think, that this was more than a simple physical correction. Even if he did not know this, his words triggered something in me, and my own innate wisdom told me to try taking some leaps, which I did. In either case, the literal and metaphorical were connected, and seeing this allows for spiritual growth, and making some good choices.

Words have power. Words are power. Metaphor is a fickle, playful, dangerous, and wise thing, frequently revealing itself, frequently revealing truths that surprise, or make us uncomfortable. But there they, truths, and we're better served facing them sooner, and working on whatever it is we need to work on, than ignoring them or scratching defensively away at them. For this, and other reasons, it is worthwhile to talk to teachers you find wise and trustworthy, and to spend some time in communities or in a community you

Selfless Self Help

find wise and trustworthy. Those things, teachers, and communities, help empower and purify our words. They show us metaphor in increasingly dazzling forms, while helping us, the students, to become less cruel, less aggressive, more compassionate. Both inner words, thoughts, and outer words can become kinder. As everyone will surely acknowledge, more kindness of words is something all communities, spiritual or otherwise, need very much.

Back to balancing

Just before this, I was talking about meditators working with energy, finding ways to use it during daily life, but not becoming overly guarded, or solid. Our permeability is important, and the ability to fortify or stabilize the mind, stabilize our spirit, doesn't mean becoming shut off to others, or the world.

Here's another way to look at this. We tend to think of people as somebodies. People are people. They have selves, made up of parts such as memories, beliefs, fears. We have likes and dislikes. When we look at ourselves, especially after having meditated for a little while, it is possible to see that the "somebody" quality is not as self-evident as might previously have been thought. To put it more clearly: our sense of somebody, for self or other, can become flexible. This flexibility is in line with the truth. To oversimplify someone is to become rigid. People are complex, and ever-changing. The flexibility I'm talking about in this context is about seeing that people are more like whirlwinds than blocks of stone. I recently found out that my employer, who is fairly uptight in his habits, and dresses in mostly white T-shirts and khakis, used to be a hippie, and hitchhiked around as a young man. I have seen old

friends get married to people I don't know and start families. I've

seen my own tastes and interest change a lot over the years, from

blues to hip hop in high school, to more pop these days, which I

would never have imagined as a youngster. People are changeable

and complex.

When Buddhists talk about emptiness or selflessness in the context

of persons, this is one thing they're talking about, and if you read

any contemporary Buddhist writing, you'll probably be reminded

that that emptiness is not nothingness. It's not that people are

voids; it's that they are not the blocks of stone or the statues that

we assume

they are so much of the time, for some reason.

The "nobody" quality is flexibility, the sense not of nothingness,

but something closer to nothingness than set in stone. So, on the

left, there is nobodiness, people as flexible and complicated, not

having a center in the normal sense, and the right, somebodiness,

the commonsense view of folks as being there. We all know the

latter view. We don't have to try to deny it or throw it out. People

are people. We experience people. In terms of balance, it seems like it makes sense to find a point between these two things: a point between something and nothing, between rock and wind.

Now, if that makes some poetic or abstract sense, that's one thing. The important point is that it makes experiential sense, in regards to living experience. What does it feel like to be somebody? It feels solid, definite. Our definitions and understandings of self and other hold up, make sense, work. Our stories about life and our path work, whether or not they are dreamy or nightmarish. What does it feel to be nobody? We are losing it. Our definitions and understanding are chaotic and confused, seeming to fall away as soon as we say them to ourselves. Our stories are constantly being called into question. Being surprised could feel this way. Getting fired, getting dumped, moving could feel this way.

The former and the latter, somebody and nobody, can work together. When we're too somebody, sacred world flees from view-things are too clear, too easy, too defined. When we're too nobody, sacred world also disappears, or maybe is an overwhelming mess. The two can be balanced, and I think this must be done in terms of experience, fueled by practice.

Think, right now, about where you feel, today, on this spectrum. Where are you right now, a somebody, or a nobody? If you look at today, where have you fallen, for the most part, which one? Have they been balanced? If so, that's something to be proud of, and if not, that's not a problem either, it just indicates where you stand right now, and possibly where you stand most of the time. That is, unless today was, for some reason, especially unusual or different from most other days.

In one way, working on loosening up habits is about both, about both becoming more of person, and becoming less stuck in a particular personality. I was thinking back to what I did today, and one thing I'm proud of is that I spent some time, at work, reading a book I like. This is a habit I've developed over the last few weeks, reading at work, on down time, and I'm pleased that I've been doing this. I had, previously, been mostly listening to podcasts on my phone. That can be good, and the two aren't mutually exclusive, but with reading, I feel like I'm enriching my mind, pushing myself forward. I have not been much of a reader for the last five or six years, and I feel like I am better for being a reader. The habit I worked to establish has made me a more interested person, in life, and this is a kind of becoming more of a person. I changed a habit, and I built up a new one. The new one didn't just loosen up the old habit, it installed something else, something I found enriching (if a little more difficult than just sitting and listening).

Thinking back over my workday, today, I also felt pretty stressed out. It was a little busy, someone had to leave early, so my coworkers and I were all moving a little faster than usual so this person could go home. It was not a terrible day, objectively speaking, but a little stressful, and I felt angry much of the time, even though I worked to stay calm and used all sorts of meditation techniques to try to turn that inner burn of irritation into something more compassionate. Looking at these negativities, at my own irritability today, this was a kind of being caught in one personality, being too much one person, not enough of a nobody. Now, if I'd been successful in being less habitual, and if I'd been successful in seeing things from my coworker's point of view, this might have been different. As a teacher once told me, you start with moments, dots, of mindfulness, and then these can be strung together, into a line. I think it works this way with being compassionate, too. It may start with short moments of seeing things from another's perspective, but eventually we need to increase that, so that our view is not a safe home, a safe couch. We are attempting to shift our home so that thinking in terms of others

173

Selfless Self Help

becomes home. And so we come back to balance. I have not had a child, but I've heard mothers talk about how the needs of others can eclipse their own, and this is not what I'm suggesting. I'm suggesting looking at when life is difficult, and how these moments might have something to teach about the somebodiness/ nobodiness combo, as well as habits and compassion.

I'm Melting, I'm Melting, What a World, What a World!

I said a little bit about my personal story, the martial arts, and the drug problems. Another part of my personal story is that, for a long time, I felt victimized. I was never the victim of anything specially horrible, like abuse or neglect. I did not grow up as part of a culture that discriminated against me because of my ethnicity. I never had to deal with the disadvantages connected to being very poor. Still, a running theme, for me, has been that I have felt like a victim, especially when things go wrong in some area of my life.

My abuse of pot and psychedelics, along with alcohol, and some other substances, I can't really put on anyone else. I did that to myself, and I've learned from it. With that, I cannot claim to be a victim. In other circumstances, like when I've been fired from jobs, or had relationships that didn't work out, it's very easy to feel like a victim. When my life doesn't measure up to my expectations of what an adult life should be, based on a million concepts gathered from all over, it's easy to feel like a victim. Our society, and I would wager most societies, has a competitive side to it, and for me, one way this shows up is feeling a kind of competition to have a good life (not just finding success and respect, but to live well as a kind of competition with everyone else, where one's experiences and happiness are the marker or whether one has won or not). So when I feel like my life is less of a life than it should be, one way this plays out is a feeling being a victim (ie, those other, happier people, have had it easier than me, my life is not good enough because I've been the victim of bad circumstances, malevolent people, and so on).

This might seem removed from a discussion of compassion, which is what I've been mostly writing about in these chapters. Here is the connection: seeing hypocrisy transform into compassion can be part of a process of taking off the shackles of victim mentality. (Let me be clear that I'm not talking about cases of actual victimization, but times when people blame the world or blame others for things that were partly or completely their own fault, and times when people develop a worldview in which being a victim is an indispensable part of how they delude themselves). Taking off the shackles of victim mentality is also part of what people call "taking responsibility."

Let's say that I'm having an argument with my wife. We are sitting in the car, and somehow we get to a discussion of when we're going to get an oil change done. The argument progresses, I notice something that bothers me about my wife, and then I maybe see it as hypocrisy, and a little compassion arises. There can be a kind of loosening that happens when you get out of a hypocritical, judging mindset, and into a more open, compassionate mindset. This is the moment, in an argument, when you allow that maybe the other person might have made some good points. This loosening is the opposite of the feeling of being a victim. Additionally, the position of judgment, seeing others as the problem, and the position of victimhood, are extremely close.

When I see the pushy people who won't get out of my way in the supermarket, I'm being something of a hypocrite. When I feel like the supermarket's hapless victim, or the hapless victim of those pushy shoppers, it's the same kind of feeling. It's nice to get out of that mindset. Here's something else: the feeling of being a victim and the emotional storyline about being the hero or underdog in one's own life are related. I don't know about everyone else, but for me, feeling like the main character in the movie of my life, feeling like a struggling protagonist, and feeling somewhat downtrodden are connected. I am not suggesting that life doesn't involve struggle, or puzzles, or real hardship, but seeing yourself as set against the world, which some people do, I do, not only makes things more challenging than they need to be, it is also an oversimplification. It means that you think everyone else is the problem. How could you be happy, or satisfied with life, feeling like everyone else out there is the real problem, and feeling like you're the victim of life?

Now, when I think about the stories of my past (and I definitely recommend that everyone do this, don't just pretend to let go of your personal past, not right away, you must begin to process it) I am a little less stuck in my feeling of being a victim of old girlfriends, or terrible bosses, or challenging situations. Honesty is essential. I'm not saying you should take on a stance of total responsibility, because there are times when others are genuinely out to get you, or when others do really try to hurt or malign you, but these times are probably less frequent than the imagination suggests.

"Do not look upon this world with fear and loathing. Bravely face whatever the gods offer." Morihei Ueshiba

For a minute, let's go back to the Tarthang Tulku idea of the bystander. The bystander is a version of the self outside of things, observing, and there is an implication or suggestion of

178

powerlessness, as is often the case with bystanders who happen to see violent or shocking events. One significant part of the bystander model is taking up positions. The bystander as separate from the world is a position, and that separation allows for certain kinds of knowledge (most kinds that we would normally think of), but also creates a kind of gap that is hard to cross over. If there is me, here, observing, then everything else is out there, and it will always be that way. All issues of potential loneliness or isolation aside, this is problematic because it means that knowing is limited by the gap. I can't know directly. I have to, from outside, investigate. This basic position supports other positions, and positions themselves are limiting in some ways, if useful. Think about politics. When someone is rabidly ensconced in one political view, they always miss out on some possibilities. If you see people on opposite sides of the political spectrum debate on TV, this is clear; it's not an exploration of various solutions, it tends to be more like a battle based on positions.

The bystander engages in positioning, and if that is done thoughtlessly, it can lead to having a closed mind. I say all of this in the context of a discussion of victim mentality for two reasons. First, isn't victim mentality a perfect example of taking up a position? The victim sees themselves as being at the mercy of larger, intractable forces, out there. Everything tends to be seen in terms of that losing battle. Sometimes glimmers of hope appear, but they eventually just become further highlights of victimhood, their glittering promises further emphasizing the hopelessness of it all. Second, positioning, of any kind, although we're using victim mentality as the example here, is not inherently unworkable. Positioning is workable. It can be explored and worked through.

The role of inquiry or questioning in TSK is something I brought up before. What is there not to like about questioning? Even better, the openness questioning invokes. I can't tell you how many times finding some openness in my mind has defused anger and stubbornness. Think about this environment of openness in terms of positions. Victimhood, and other stories or interpretations of our life, are positions. We can look at them, and see if they have some wisdom. What do they have to offer? A first step is distancing ourselves from the addictive power of those identifications (I'm a victim, or I'm a hero, I'm a good person who always does things the proper way, really any strong storyline). The next step is, I think, going beyond even that distancing, and allowing stories and positions to be what they are, then allowing ourselves to play with them. This takes one from the bystander, in which positioning is a given, and knowledge is more limited, to a freer view. One interesting coincidence is that, during my drug years, I was very much a bystander, on the outside, yet also stuck inside my mind, not powerful enough to take the necessary steps to interact. As I came out of that phase, martial arts were very helpful and transformative, and the opposite of bystander mentality- all about interacting, reaching out, making contact. As some people like to phrase it, it's about "connecting."

Selfless Self Help

A Little Reminder About Goodness

I want to reiterate one thing. While looking at victim mentality, judgment, and hypocrisy, it is normal for people to become self-critical, and this self-directed looking can become aggressive very easily. (Criticism has great value, and meditators would get nowhere if not for some healthy criticism; it's more about the aggression or hate that seems to attach itself to criticism that's problematic.)

Becoming compassionate, or letting your naturally occurring inherent compassion blossom, however you want to put it, should be, at least part of the time, pleasant. It should not be a self flagellating process, even if you end up noticing a lot of hidden faults and neurosis along the way. It should be pleasant because it is not a waste of time. (So many activities really are, and life is precious, so wasting time is not to be taken lightly. Cheryl Richardson's Self Care talks about this, sometimes in terms of protecting your own energy.) It should be pleasant because it is freeing, in groundlessness. It should be pleasant because you are becoming better able to understand and cope with real world scenarios (as opposed to the difficulty that arises when you're

182

trying to cope and understand from a more victim oriented, uncompassionate perspective). On a little bit larger scale, most, if not all, techniques and practices seem to be about unblocking the flow of emotional energy, and all natural energies, so that life can flow well, and so that there is less blockage, and less clumsiness. Becoming a more compassionate person should, I think, also contribute to this: releasing stale old thought patterns about being attacked, or about the wrongness of other people can't help but make the mind less stagnant. If you want an example of stagnancy, talk to someone who repeats themselves ad nauseam. Then, think of someone who is able to respond with freshness and spontaneity to a wide array of occurrences and topics. That sparkling responsiveness of the latter example is worth keeping in mind- not that we have to be sparkly and cheerful all the time, but that stagnancy (think cocoon) is not what we are aiming for, and most times, it is not far off. Stagnancy is not pleasant. Getting things moving and flowing will not always be fun or easy, but it does feel more right than its opposite, the shell.

Part of the trick seems to be finding some way to be positive, while knowing about cocoon, and all the other negatives. Personally, I've been finding that a lot of people spend much of their time watching the news and getting upset about it; there are a lot of negatives out

Selfless Self Help

there. In relation to balancing out the training in compassion, a reminder about basic goodness might be in order.

Certainly we should take our lives seriously, but that doesn't mean driving ourselves to the brink of disaster or complaining about our problems or holding a grudge against the world. We have to accept personal responsibility for uplifting our lives. When you don't punish or condemn yourself, when you relax more and appreciate your body and mind, you begin to contact the fundamental notion of basic goodness in yourself. (Trungpa, Shambhala)

There is so much to say about this quote, but, as someone once very accurately observed, when I begin to explain these things line by line, often the sense of power seems to vanish. I will say a few things, though. Taking life seriously means living a meaningful life. The whole aim of Selfless Self Help is to aid people in this pursuit. At the same time, that search for meaning, and the process is stirring meaning into as much of everyday activities as possible, can create tension and frustration, which is usually counterproductive.

Eventually, and I have experienced this, over time, as you practice meditation consistently, and as you practice trying to be spontaneous and kind, you can start to appreciate things more. Part of this idea of goodness is that life, and all of the amazing details and moments that make up "life," can be appreciated. In fact, when

184

it comes to meaning and not wasting time, appreciation is one of
the best things to do. Without appreciation, what is there? With
appreciation, real appreciation, life is lived.

So, this kind of goodness makes sense. If your mind is going a
mile a minute, and you feel confused, it's very easy to lose sight of
it, and even to come up with sophisticated logical objections to it.
If something very surprising happens, or if you wear yourself out a
little by doing something very physical, it can become easier to see
this kind of simple goodness. However, there is something
strangely sophisticated and difficult to grasp about it. Trungpa
writes, later in Shambhala, "when we speak of basic goodness, we
are not taking about having allegiance to good and rejecting bad.
Basic goodness is good because it is unconditional, or
fundamental." So goodness is not just some superficial way to prop
up self esteem when the training gets harsh or when you get down
on yourself; it is very profound. This kind of profundity is
something I'd like to talk more about in the next section of the
book, after a discussion of the goals of habit practice and
compassion practice.

Pema Chodron puts it this way: "There's a reason you can learn
from everything: you have basic wisdom, basic intelligence, and

basic goodness." These truths are simple, yet hard to unfold. Think about how life is a learning process. This is one thing that's happening if we are looking at, possibly denigrating ourselves; we're learning. Pema is suggesting that there's a reason we can learn, and it has a lot to do with basic goodness. In other words, seeing problems doesn't make them unsolvable. Let's also remember that, by practicing and trying to be decent folks, we're doing something immensely valuable. That is goodness too.

Goals, Again

Applied in our own lives, a knowledge that dissolved our suffering would be a gift more precious than any other. (Tarthang Tulku, LON)

Two goals: spontaneity and compassion. That is the point of this chapter. After spinning off into stories or examples or other ideas, it's good to come back to simplicity. Practice every day, even if just for a little while. Apply the teachings on habit and hypocrisy, and then measure your experiences against them. Without too much self deprecation (which is contrary to confidence, and confidence is a marker of wisdom) check your life against the lofty ideals of being spontaneous, and being nonjudgmentally compassionate. It is fairly easy to agree with ideas about spiritual progress, or maturity, but I think everyone probably has many times in their life when here seems to be a hidden momentum propelling them towards negativity. Those very situations are the ones in which we need to apply meditation, habit training, and nonhypocrisy.

One popular technique coming out of popular culture, and I apologize if one individual came up with this and I'm not giving them credit, but it's very commonly known, is to say "yes." This is one that, for years, seemed too cheesy to be worth my time. A lot of positivity type approaches seem superficial or fake to me, a lot of the time, so I don't usually gravitate toward them. The idea is, with saying yes, that people get caught in a habit of saying "no" to things automatically, and this creates a cocoon, limits their life. Here is how I've found this useful.

When my wife used to suggest something that caught me off guard, like going to a restaurant I hadn't been thinking about, or going somewhere I'm not totally interested in, I tended to say no, or think it over a lot. I wanted to negotiate. Negotiation is very valuable, but I found that with a lot of these circumstances, I could say yes pretty quickly, and things went okay. If I felt really against going to a certain Chinese buffet, for example, I could say so. Most of the time, when this kind of thing came up, though, a simple quick yes was very workable. Like I said before, I see a lot of the path as being about flow, getting things flowing when they've been stuck, and in this case, I found a way to get things flowing a little more. I think the idea of saying yes, or as some folks say, "saying yes to life," has some nuances and complications to it. I'm sure others have tackled this, some with good ideas.

Spontaneity. Flow. Life is full of movement and energy, and part of this is stagnant, churning places. Those places are what we're looking to attack with using habits to invoke spontaneity. This reminds me of a time when I was with my family, on vacation, at some beach. It might've been Cape Cod in Massachusetts. We were walking, and we passed by a whirlpool. It was medium sized, but it looked furiously powerful to me, as a child, and it was tearing off chunks of the beach, chunks of sand. I started yelling to my parents, who, a little annoyed, said its okay, it's fine, just walk around it. It seemed so powerful.

Times when the momentum of time propel us into confusion and misery are like this whirlpool. You could say that both ideas, that this whirlpool is no big deal, and that it is terrifying, are true. Arguing and tension and pain are commonplace. They are to be worked with, no big deal there. The reason they are to be worked with is that they are powerful. If they were not, they would not induce pain in self and other.

Just to finish this section I want to reiterate the value of practice and training (and group training, at least sometimes). Some people are more comfortable working on their habits and bringing out compassion, but less comfortable sitting consistently. Some people

Selfless Self Help

are comfortable sitting every day, but less comfortable working on

getting out of their rut and out of their hypocrisy.

Karlins

Selfless Self Help

Section three

Mind

Entry into the Sacred

People often say, "Meditation is all very well, but what does it
have to do with my life?" What it has to do with your life is that
perhaps through this simple practice of paying attention – giving
loving-kindness to your speech and your actions and the moments
of your mind – you begin to realize that you're always standing in
the middle of a sacred circle, and that's your whole life...Everyone
who walks up to you has entered that sacred space, and it's not an
accident. Whatever comes into the space is there to teach you...
Our life's work is to use what we have been given to wake up...to
let the things that enter into the circle wake you up rather than put
you to sleep...You can leave your marriage, you can quit your job,
you can go where people are going to praise you...but the same old
demons will always come up until finally you have learned your
lesson, the lesson they came to teach you. Then those same
demons will appear as friendly, warmhearted companions on the
path. Pema Chodron, the Wisdom of No Escape

"Our way is not to sit to acquire something; it is to express our true

nature. That is our practice." Shunryu Suzuki

Is meditation the way to introduce ourselves to sacredness? Is

meditation an end in itself? Yes.

192

It is snowing heavily outside. A blizzard, as they say.

I did a bit of shoveling earlier, and will do some more soon.

It was somewhat enjoyable (although it would feel very different if I did it every day, or if I had to do it for hours). Just sitting in front of my Tv, which I do sometimes, is so often unsatisfying. A million things could be said about the "meaningful life," and what is meaning, after all? Maybe that question is as unhelpful as most of the philosophy that has been built up over time, to discuss the logical ins and outs of what living a good life is. I think there is a feeling of true satisfaction that goes along with meaningful activities that is hard to argue with. I felt this after shoveling.

The upcoming section is "mind." After delving a little more into the mysteries of Tarthang Tulku's TSK, we will talk about mind, which is the most esoteric part of this training. Habits are pretty down to earth. Not easy to work on, but relatively straightforward. Compassion, and the difficulties of being in the world and being with others, still pretty straightforward. Once we get to mind, though, it gets not only more esoteric, but problematic; why even bother with that? If we can get out of ruts, and become kinder

193

people, why even bother with the more mysterious, sublime, philosophical aspects of life? Allow me to return to the quotes I began the chapter with.

This training, Selfless Self Help, could be said to be about meditation: developing consistent practices, and incorporating those practices into daily life experiences. I am confident that, although there is clearly a Buddhist background to this system, it is accessible and useful to many faiths.

"Meditation is all very well, but what does it have to do with my life?"

Pema answers this by talking about a view, and an experience of the sacredness of life, which is the same thing as the meaningfulness of life. Being present, in the present, which is supported by practicing some sort of spiritual discipline daily, can become an experience of what she called realizing "that you're always standing in the middle of a sacred circle." This, to me, sounds just like the quote from Suzuki Roshi. Is it something we acquire, or something innate? To make those distinctions, or argue over them is probably a waste of time. At various points, the intersection between experience and philosophical concepts becomes beyond words, and words can become intoxicating, in either a positive or negative way. The idea of something being "beyond words" is something I'll try to touch on in the next section. Here is another way to talk about his: there are levels of language. What we call being beyond words usually means that other, less obvious, levels of language, or layers of language are at play. When that is the case, it can be good to address those. A basic example would be the kind of intuitive feeling out that happens so much of the time in conversation. In the silences and pauses, there is a lot of language. We can't discuss or appreciate or understand the sacred without some acceptance of this form of language. I have no final understandings to share when it comes to the mind, or to the flow of language in the world, but I do want to try to talk about them a little. Waking up involves spontaneity and compassion, but also language. Talking about mind, in this training, means talking about language.

Expressing our true nature, and waking up- these concepts push you in the direction of something I call here sacredness (which I get from Trungpa, of course). The work on habits, and hypocrisy seem to be separate from this stuff, this more spacey high level stuff, but they are not. The cocoon has a lot to do with creating separations and boundary and containedness when it should not be

195

created. Hypocrisy and judgment do the same things. Living a meaningful life, one in harmony with the sacred, has everything to do with understanding, dancing with, transforming, applying strategies to, appreciating, those boundaries, and separations. We can't say, actually, that we're entering into the sacred now, because it happened at the very beginning, but it is becoming more vivid now, as the appreciation of the holiness of the world reverberates, or accumulates, like snow. (In truth, I'm rewriting this now, in the Spring, so it's odd and interesting for me to read about snow, now. The seasons change, and I keep writing. Living with the seasons is one thing coming up in the next section. As I've been applying these teachings to my own life, over the last few years, I have seen both that certain feelings and energies go along with each season, and that there's also a feeling that nothing changes, that those natural movements are an illusion.)

It is not necessary to believe this, and I could be wrong, really. But I am trying to be honest, and this is my experience. As Pema says, we can realize things by just paying attention.

Karlins

The Meditator's World

We're beginning to talk about entering the meditator's world, the world of spirit. This happens gradually. The more you meditate, the more your mind and your energy change. You become more open to sense experiences. Sensations that were just barely perceptible before can become more prominent.

I guess you could say there are two extremes with regards to spirit: on one end of the spectrum, there are rationalist science types. For them, energy is a word that means nothing, and confuses the issue. Meditation is mind training, and any talk of metaphysical seeming realities is nonsense. There's a lot to this, and the hardheadedness of it has some merit, I think. On the other end of the spectrum are New Age types, people who have no problem using crystals one day, making decisions based on astrology the next. As much as I find fault with this kind of perspective, there's something to it as well; New Age practices, although they tend to be too much about picking and choosing, less than rigorous, are about magic, and magic has always been, and will always be a part of culture (and not at the level of clear rituals and codified practices, although

197

those can be good, but at the basic, inescapable level, where superstition and slightly illogical, or arational, behavior shape people's actions on a daily basis). Intuition is a deeply rooted part of most people's lives, and this is what unacknowledged magic deals with- avoiding certain people just based on a vibe or feeling, frequenting places for similar reasons. Unacknowledged magic, unacknowledged intuition shape the human life like winds shape sand dunes on a beach. Everyone sees the sand hills, everyone walks on them, but for some reason we don't think about it. Maybe thinking about it would change it, or make it disappear.

These self-hidden truths are matters of language and matters of energy. Energy is a way of talking about mind (in terms of feelings, the way things are associated and interact, and what could be called the paranormal). Mind would include talking about energy, too. They're just two angles from which to address one issue, from that perspective. Or look at it as a trio, mind, energy, language.

Systems that look at energy as simply a physical phenomena, or a health matter, are too limited. Sadly, some people might connect more easily with this kind of description, as opposed to a description of reality. We started off by talking about habits, which

198

is really an ongoing thing. I don't think it's a good idea to give up looking at your habits and where you get stuck. That should continue on as long as you are a meditator. One huge reason for this is the fact that it's so hard to overcome habituation; it's so entrenched. It would be one thing if you were able to see that habits are addictive, they have this pull to them, and then you cultivated some spontaneity and everything cleared up. Unfortunately, it doesn't seem to work that way, at least not for most of us.

It hasn't for me! What has happened, at this point, is that I've gotten a lot more cognizant of when I'm being habitual, and when I'm able to make that leap. Sometimes it takes others to pull us out of our shells. When I'm being cowardly, sometimes I'll run across someone else who will do this, and I'm grateful for that.

In terms of habits, there's plenty of energy experience to look at. There is the energy of addiction, the feeling of being seduced by some comforting experience. This is not centered completely in one person, although individuals are somehow held responsible anyway, which seems a little unfair. If you're around a lot of people who are very asleep, or addicted to various things, this will tend to rub off on you. It's not just that you're influenced by their words or actions, there's something less substantial, which we call "energy." If you're in a group of people who love to gamble, you might find yourself thinking about gambling a lot more. It's not that your mind has suddenly, randomly, shifted into this state of consciousness; their energy has affected you. When you're with this group of gamblers, you could even notice your voice, your body language, posture all changing slightly to become more like them. What people call body language is closely joined with energy.

With this way of describing energy, I'm talking about something very large. Smaller, more concentrated experiences are easier to understand, probably. A smaller experience of this energy happens in your body, and your mind, your personal mind. Right now I'm thinking about eating dessert. That minor addiction, the desire, has a feeling to it. It feels sort of magnetic, and small to me. When I pay attention to my breathing there's a certain feeling of breathing that goes along with it too. It probably feels a little different to other people. The stronger the emotion, the more bodily palpable the experience of energy. Panic, intense fear, rage, overwhelming lust, crushing depression, these all have feelings that go with them. There is flow, direction, movement, even warmth or coldness. Is it real? It doesn't matter in this context. It is consistent- personal, but consistent. It is common to consider emotions as groups of thought patterns, which is true, but we can't ignore the energetic side of anger, happiness, surprise, et cetera. So, it's possible to understand emotional instances as energetic, but I'm arguing against limiting "energy" to that. It is not as small or personal as those physical experiences. It extends to environments, others, groups. It can change based on a person, but also within a small area, or a large area, over a season, like weather. When you observe these larger movements, sometimes you can perceive less common sense types of energy manifesting, the kind of things that mystics talk about (and we don't need to force that as some kind of enlightenment experience, but it is there, it is traditional and there for a reason, namely, because it is real).

At that point, the question of the self comes back. What kind of self is it that can be molded and shifted by the energy of other beings, by the energy of groups? Do groups themselves have a self of sorts? People will sometimes talk about "group energy." A certain bunch of people has a very speedy, intellectual energy, while another group might have a depressed, sad energy. I don't want to oversimplify and say that some are good, some bad, but this is a way to understand what I mean when I talk about energy. There are feelings involved, and associations of phenomena. As we

Selfless Self Help

more fully enter the meditator's world of experience, energy and new knowledge of the self can arise. I'm clearly not talking in a precise way here about selves, or about subtle energy, and that is what it is like as your mind expands, through prayer, not usually precise, but gradually more open.

So-Called Negative Energies

For one thing, it would be really interesting to contemplate what people, places, things, call up "positive energy" for you. This doesn't have to be especially New Agey or esoteric. It could be a bookstore, or a bar, or someone you know you has an atmosphere of calm around them. I think one question that spins off from there is: how much of this has to do with your biases, neurosis, self-deception, andhow much of it is something real? A drug addict might say, at first, that their dealer brings up positive feelings.

One perspective on the matter is that there are, speaking broadly, environments that tend to be positive energetically, and environments that tend to be negative energetically. This is personal; some people's pleasant town is another's boring nowhere. There are things to be learned from both. Being in negative environments can teach you things about stabilizing your mind, being unbiased, and fearlessness. Being in positive environments is refreshing, and can teach you about beauty and friendliness.

Selfless Self Help

To go back to the problem of habit, what can we make of the energies of claustrophobia, pain, and limitation? How do you work with the feeling of claustrophobia? I think there are a lot of different approaches to this, mostly based on the practice of meditation. I think it is possible to come up with a lot of your own, personal ways to deal with this kind of negative feeling, but the more it's based on the personal practice of meditation, the better. Meditation provides solid grounding in experience. Without it, things easily get ungrounded.

Whether things are refreshing, exciting, horrifying, or disappointing, it's essential to come back to the groundedness meditation shows. There's a back and forth, a positive feedback loop, between that groundedness, and the lightshows of energy the world provides to us.

It starts with the mind of meditation. This mind can be invoked whenever and wherever. It's often difficult, but it can be done. Millions of practitioners, of all traditions, have done this, and many times in the most unpleasant, harsh circumstances. What you can do is apply your meditation, and your meditation experience, directly, to the experience of energy. Working with breathing and sensations are good, basic ways to do this (but so powerful that they keep being useful even years after you've first learned them, they're not basic in the sense that you can forget them once you've been at it for a little while).As you progress on the path, whatever path, you're working on the basics. There's no end to work on the basic principles. Having mastered the basics is a sign that you've attained complete realization.

Another suggestion is to investigate as far as possible when you're encountering negative energies, or seemingly negative energies. There can be so much there. Sometimes a lot of it is just a projection or reaction based on your own conditioning. Very often what seems to happen is someone reacts or projects based on a neurotic interpretation, and then that actually begins to shape the reality of the situation. There's an interplay between delusion and reality, and especially when you don't want to step out of delusion, there's the desire to make reality conform to your nightmares, and to ignore the complexities of it not conforming entirely.

This is a potentially confusing point. First, what I'm saying is that when we perceive an energy or environment as unpleasant, sometimes it's accurate, but sometimes it's more about our own assumptions and fears than the actual raw direct experience of said energy. Second, this relates to our conditioning. Third, once an interpretation has taken hold somewhat, which happens pretty fast, it doesn't end there. The interpretation has a life of its own, an energy of its own, which flavors things. Then, that flavoring process seep into the moment and influences things on a slightly less subtle level. Often, I think, the neurotic interpretation flavors reality, which then becomes somewhat like the misinterpretation, and then we end up seeing that polluted reality as confirmation of what we first misperceived- it was true all along (we think). Finally, this tends to shore up our conditioning, fears, worldviews, and habits of seeing. It is no wonder that it takes so long, and so much work to get past ourminds' ruts.

Your mind is not bound to intellectual exercises, reasoning, memories, or normative sensations. Your mind can expand into the body, out into the environment, and do many things you didn't know it could do. We call this working with energy, or working with the mind. Becoming morecognizant of negative energies and negative experiences is a very good way to open this door. This freedom is key. Knowing it on an intellectual level and realizing it are far apart, but just knowing it intellectually is something. It really is. This is one reason the fear of mental unrest or insanity must be overcome as much as possible, because in order to work with the wide range of energies in the universe, to experience things beyond what is normatively allowed to us or assumed, like a false straitjacket, we need to have some confidence that we're not just going to fall apart. We need to understand that there is much more to sanity than we'd imagined, and we need to have the practical, earthy skills of meditation in order to right ourselves when things do get ugly, which they will, sometimes.

Selfless Self Help

The Energy of Language

Working with language is a vast and interesting gateway into the energetic world. One more traditional approach to this has been chanting or reciting religious texts. In the classes we do contemplation practice, which is similar. I think almost any method that works with language, spoken or written, accesses energy.

This puts the problem of thinking in a certain perspective. If many people come to meditation expecting to destroy or subjugate their thoughts, and if thoughts seem to be made in large part of language, then the "thinking problem" has something to do with language. This is not to suggest that some superficial solution exists in terms of language, like just thinking nice thoughts, somehow, or simply altering the language we encounter. What I'm suggesting is that the energy associated with language and the processes language becomes enmeshed with is important to thought, and that these things, working to transform deeply our problematic and painful thought processes, and learning to work with the energy of language, are inseparable. I am suggesting that the road to enlightenment is paved with language. Maybe it is worth considering that language and energy are the same thing at some level, or different facets of the same thing.

There are numerous implications. One is intuitive. When you hear someone speaking, or read someone's words, you can pick up on certain things seemingly between or around or underneath the language. This involves sensing with the heart.

Without being overly biased or simplistic, words seem to carry and dance with energies. The music you listen to, the entertainment you take in, who you spend time with and communicate with, all have an impact on your experience of language, and your energy. This is especially important when it comes to spiritual instruction and study. Reading a lousy novel is one thing. Immersing yourself in lousy, watered-down spiritual junk is not only a waste of time, it's a sure way to create more confusion and suffering. Spending a lot of time on this kind of material is actually a defense mechanism, most of the time, a way of avoiding real, down to earth study of texts transmitted from genuine wisdom traditions (and there are quite a few real ones). It's ego's way of coopting the journey, offering sidetracks.

Selfless Self Help

Knowing the difference between good and bad books, good teachers and bad ones, is a matter of experience and opinion. There are many criteria, and many criteria based on the particular tradition you're engaged with. There should not be a feel of extreme cluttered complexity, or clumsy intellectualism. There should not be a lot of promises or guarantees of easy answers. The more security and the more a sort of soothing spiritual lullaby something offers, the more suspect it is.

On top of the energetic promise of language, with its beauty, and also its seductively confusing quality, there is the problem of capturing. Just like photographs, language never captures reality. There is a dance between the living and dancing quality of language, and reality beyond language, the electric silence of reality. You can't say reality is nonconceptual, or is entirely conceptual. Look at how language fits with, and also misses what is really happening, in a moment.

This relates, also, to seeking out good spiritual instruction: how skilled is the author or teacher at navigating this dance of language and reality? This is important.

Turning the eye inward

When you have practiced consistently for a little while (and please try it with a group, I really wish I had sooner; it helps tremendously) perceptions can sharpen, and eventually perceiving energy becomes clearer. Sensing energy is normal, ordinary, and meditation brings it more to the surface. When you're sitting next to someone and you "feel" what sort of emotional state they're in, that's energy. It's fascinating, and also ordinary.

I'd like to describe, if I can, something I've come to think of as "turning the eye inward." It's basically a way of describing the process of perceiving energy. It has to do with intuition. I find that energy and intuition usually go together. (Because I also find that my intuition is flawed, I think it's good to say that we have to be careful with intuition. It's easily confused with bias, and delusion.)

When you pick up on something or someone's energy, there's an initial experience of it as a kind of sense. I think this can happen in many ways. Sometimes it's a feeling in the body, a feeling that seems to have drifted across space, from the thing to you, like a perfume. For me, oftentimes, it's a visual form. Things and beings exude light of a kind, I guess you'd call it. It's not light in the same way that a light bulb exudes light, but that's the closest analogy I can think of right now.

It could be strong or weak, chaotic or orderly, its movement could include a whole variety of things: going inward as a kind of magnetism or sinking, going outward and radiating, a flow that moves from one particular area to another, different kinds of pulses or rhythmic motions. Unfortunately, since I'm more or less self-taught when it comes to this, I don't have a system or a clear way of describing it. I do think that learning about art helped me build this ability, and when people have a good eye for visual art, or a good ear for poetry, they're beginning to learn what I'm talking about. (I should say that by "beginning to learn" I don't mean to imply mastery on my part, or that most art appreciators are lacking skill; I just think there are some differences between the kind of energy noticing I'm describing and what most people do when they look at a painting, for instance. Again, they are connected.)

So the noticer picks up on the energy from, let's say, a building. He stands in front of the building, and the energy comes to him. At that point, there's a good overall picture of the energy, I think, a "first thought" of energy. That first intuition tends to be accurate. At the

same time, it is probably not totally detailed. It could be fleshed

out more.

The person has a first notion of the energy and sees how it moves. Then he begins to think about it, question it, look at it more carefully. Turning the eye inward happens when, the first notion having happened, the person notices both the energies, his own stream of consciousness reactions/chatter in the background, and works with the interaction of the two.

The initial noticing is less conceptual, but is followed quickly by conceptual thoughts. Maybe the building's energy seems fairly strong, vibrant, and negative. That perception happens in a flash. Then the man, wanting to get to know it better, looks deeper. He keeps his mind on the energy, and pays attention to his intuition-tinged thoughts. It's strong. It is negative. Is it negative in the style of violence? No, but aggression, it does seem a little aggressive. Is it chaotic? No, it doesn't feel or look chaotic, but aggressive; it's fairly organized, just fast, rushing, and not entirely pleasant. It seems like there are some areas where that energy is stronger, like the doors, for instance. So, we go from an initial insight and

213

perception, to a more intricate look at what is going on. Turning the eye inward is about navigating that process. I hope my fairly clumsy example has served its function. The turning inward of the eye is about taking an initial glimpse of energy, and using discursive thought to deepen it. Because discursive thought can be hard to wrangle, addictive, deluded, it is important that you have a solid meditation practice first, a grounding practice, before you try this kind of thing out. As a language matter, turning the eye is about different sorts of language- the first thought of seeing, the analysis and chatter of examining it, the play between the beginning glimpse or vibe and the more conceptual labels it attracts. Language has something to do with play, back and forth. One of the big things about becoming a meditator is learning that you can direct your mind in different ways. It's rarely easy, but can be done. When talking about language, one thing we are dealing with is the subtleties or directing one's own mind. The mind is not just a straight line of words. When we work with it, we work with many layers, intricacies, worlds even. The work on language, energy, weird worlds of perception, is partly about learning to work with mind in more careful, involved ways. When we are just learning to pray, our tool set is like a hammer, we can only hammer things. As we grow and learn, we begin to have more and finer tools.

Karlins

Selfless Self Help

Plants and animals

It's a cliche, but a true one, that animals tend to feel energy when humans are too numb or distracted to. You probably know what I'm talking about already, but for the sake of argument, here's an example. You come home from work, after a busy and stressful day (not horrible, just averagely stressful). Your cat picks up on that stress and tension seeping out of you, and bolts as soon as you come in. Maybe you thought you were doing okay, but your pet's reaction tells you that you have a little work to do before the energy of that day actually transforms into something nicer to be around.

I don't have any brilliant insights to offer in terms of animals and plants, just that, for people interested in energy work, looking at them can be helpful. It's also interesting. I find it fascinating to look at things in nature. It's not about the kind of appreciation that's forced or unreal, like the way I look at sunsets sometimes, and then get bored and do something else (I'd be really surprised if I met someone who spent a long time looking at sunsets). It's the kind of appreciation that happens naturally, and I'd probably spend a lot more time gazing at flowers and trees if I wasn't afraid of people thinking I was crazy.

It is possible that, as we get more confident as practitioners, and as we experience more, we could do things that seem a little crazy. This is because we're feeling things "normal" people deny or miss, and because we're starting to not worry so much about being normal at all. I can remember, vaguely, being much younger and feeling stuck in some social setting, maybe it was a family gathering or with friends and acquaintances, and having to form my face into a smile or hide my discomfort when I was unhappy, and the soreness I felt after doing this for a time. I read somewhere that someone who'd spent significant time with the Dalai lama said that his moods were extremely changeable; he could be laughing one moment, very serious the next. The article pointed this out as a way we can be. It is not necessarily unhealthy to have changing moods, and we don't need to hide them behind some façade of stability or normalcy. In this same line of thinking, if I look at the sky, and it is absolutely amazing, as I walk into a parking lot, I don't really have to hide this or stop looking for two seconds, or ten seconds, or longer. I started by writing about plants and animals. You can sense tremendous energy in the world of plants and animals. Tuning your perceptions into this, you can go past the

217

normative. If you notice something about the natural world, you can begin to have faith in this and your ability to perceive. As Trungpa often said, first thought is best thought. So, over time (more or less, depending on who we are) we can begin to trust ourselves. Most animals seem to, and this is one thing we could learn from them.

Looking more

When someone speaks, or communicates in any way that uses words, it's more than just the words. Is this energy that we tune into, when we notice the words around the words? I don't know if there's a simple answer for that. When someone looks beyond the surface words or gestures, they look for what's going on underneath, for deeper levels of meaning. If that is not energy, what is it?

It is totally commonplace to do this. If you're buying a car, you have to try to guess what is really going on, behind the show the salesperson is putting on (because you know that their pitch and their negotiation is not entirely above-board).

In this way, reading energy, if you want to think of it that way, is about the commonplace way we have of looking more, looking under things, to be able to get more clarity, make better decisions, understand situations with more wisdom. Everyone works with energy. Everyone lives in an energetic world.

Selfless Self Help

I think of this, usually, as "listening." You can listen to what someone is "saying" when they are not talking at all. People say they "get a sense" of what someone is feeling or what kind of person they or what they might do if x happens. This kind of idiom indicates both the common human use of intuition, and how, for many of us, it is not something we want to address directly. It is accepted, to "get a sense" of things, but not, at the same time. If someone says, "I got the sense that she was upset, ready to explode," you'd know just what they meant. If you questioned it, though, asking why, what signs indicated this, what sort of sense it really was, it might create a problem. The speaker might think you were doubting them, or being overly logical, or just had a poor sense of social dynamics. Another potential issue might just be that we all use sense, intuition, all the time, and don't really know how it works, and yet we use it, have faith in it.

I remember saying something about intuition in a group class once, and the teacher, someone I respect, said something like "Intuition comes from a quiet mind." That's not it exactly, but something to that effect. I don't think that your mind needs to be crystal clear to use intuition. Obviously, people use it all day long, and their minds are rarely that clear or steady. (That's one reason we practice meditating.) But the idea is that a certain level is clarity is needed to distinguish actual feelings of intuition from chatter or "discursiveness." They can seem very close. They're all thoughts, kinds of thoughts. I think the choice of the word feeling is telling, about as close as I can get right now. When you think, it is near-aural, you can almost hear it. It is linguistic. When you have a sense, it is more of a feeling, and you can tune those feelings, look for them, direct them towards people and places, so it's not pure reaction, but it also has a different tone in the mind than the thinking of "what will I do next?" or "I remember when..."

Patterns

Recently, over the last few years, I've found it helpful to educate myself about Chinese medical theory, and what's known as "five element theory." There are a lot of reasons for this, one being that I want to be healthy without having to rely on a doctor. Another is that I want to understand the seasons, and the natural patterns of energy moving through the world. There are books by better-informed people than me about five element theory. So I think that studying that a little could be interesting for people who want to learn more about energy. To sum up my approach, though, the idea is that the seasons follow this natural progression.

The five elements describe, and can be used to describe, just about anything, but the seasons are one traditional application. One element, one season, exhibits its characteristics (the warmth of Spring, the busy-ness and expansiveness of Summer) and then changes into something else. These transformations are described by the way the five elements of water, fire, air, earth, and wood turn into one another.

It's not the only model out there, just one that's been time tested, and that I find works for me. The interesting thing is that the logic of the seasons seems to work, even though it's not scientific in the same way as biology or chemistry. The seasons change, and they all have certain atmospheres to them, certain associations. For me, each season has feelings associated with it, and not sentimental ones, but visceral feelings, energies, that arise with those seasons (and, in a small way, if I remember them or fantasize about them). Along with those feelings, it's said that specific emotions tend to pop in the context of this cycle. Feelings of tenderness and loneliness are associated with onetime of the year. It's not quite that your feelings are entirely personal, and psychological. They have something to do with the movement of energy through the earth, as time happens, as the natural world breathes and shifts.

It could be helpful to look at traditional models which describe change and patterns. This goes back to the importance of time, in TSK. One thing a lot of Buddhist theories do is just describe patterns of change over time. If you investigate your own life, you will probably find that this is real, that things really do seem to follow odd patterns, cycles. But investigating is key here. Finding some esoteric explanation and buying in wouldn't necessarily be helpful. It's also more fun to discover these things for yourself.

223

Selfless Self Help

Teacher and teachers

Finding a wisdom teacher, or teachers, is one of the strangest, scariest, most rewarding things you could do. And it must be a living person. For a few years after I started meditating, I avoided group meditation. It was scary. I avoided meditation/spiritual teachers. The whole thing seemed weird, foreign. In spite of how certain I was that I would meditate every day for the rest of my life, after having started, I was wary of the social aspect of the whole mess, and theteachers.

Within a few years, I had taken a class through my college, with a sort of eccentric dance teacher, who'd also studied philosophy, and was a practicing meditator. Of course, I'd taken college classes on philosophy and theology, and had endless discussions with friends about the meaning of life and so on, that was pretty easy. I knew that going to actual places where people practiced together, and talking to teachers was key, somehow, and that my cowardice was holding me back, so I did that.

I found one center, then another. My experiences were mixed, and in the beginning it was really very anxiety producing and uncomfortable. At some point, my experience of meditating, my whole way of seeing things, began to subtly change, and I got hooked. I would go to the Shambhala Meditation Center in New York, where I was living at the time, and every time, I think, something interesting would happen. There were wise people there. I could feel it. (Not all of them, notin the same way, but some people there had something; I could feel it, something magical.)

My first real experiences working with teachers happened there. One teacher told me to "slow down," which sticks with me to this day. (One interesting thing about this kind of instruction is that it usually changes over time, as you contemplate it and apply it to your life. The meaning could seem pretty clear at first, but then, years later, it could yield new ideas and insights.) Another teacher teased me about being "obsessive." I worked directly with a meditation teacher, and was able to ask hundreds of questions about practicing sitting, and about life in general. I'm grateful to them.

Aside from being able to brag about having "worked with teachers," those interactions had an effect on me. That's the big reason I would recommend it. My meditation practice before this time was much weaker. My whole sense of the teachings, of being a spiritual person and the possibilities of realization, were so much weaker, so tinged by my own misconceptions. As one example of this, I tried to do a little meditation retreat on my own, when I was living in California, and failed. I set out to meditate for a whole day, in my room, and got through maybe an hour and a half or two hours. Then I jumped up, in frustration. It was off. I couldn't stand the boredom and anxiety.

It was a good idea, but I didn't have the knowledge, or the strength of mind, or the sense of the teachings, to do a retreat. While in NewYork, a year or so later, I did a workshop with a group of people. That made it possible. Taking a workshop made it possible to sit for a few hours in a day, and then the benefits of that extended sitting came into existence. I'm saying this because I think a lot of people, and unfortunately, people who have been practicing for a very long time, avoid group practice and teachers. They stay on their own, practicing their way, and not benefiting from what communities and instructors provide.

Selfless Self Help

It is possible to learn things on your own, such as calming the mind, visualizing, and physical forms like yoga. It's possible to learn parts of those systems. You will go off track, though. Everyone does, with or without the support of community. The good thing about having recourse to a community is that you're not stuck in that trap, once you fall in. You can find the way out, and then keep going, making progress.

Sand Castle

We are like children building a sand castle. We embellish it with beautiful shells, bits of driftwood, and pieces of colored glass. The castle is ours, off limits to others. We're willing to attack if others threaten to hurt it. Yet despite all our attachment, we know that the tide will inevitably come in and sweep the sand castle away. The trick is to enjoy it fully but without clinging, and when the time comes, let it dissolve back into the sea. (Pema Chödrön, When Things Fall Apart: Heart Advice for Difficult Times)

My first real foray into the world of practice was when I started learning martial arts. I think for a lot of men, this serves multiple functions: it is spiritual, physical, practical, and also helps us understand and define ourselves as men. This is not a small part of it, and it was meaningful for me, defining my own masculinity. I would never say that every man needs to learn how to fight, but for a lot of men, it is a very primal, instinctual desire that gets filtered through cultural lenses. Depending on where you live, being a man and being able to fight, or defend, are more or less connected. Growing up, as I did, in a very nonviolent, intellectual, artsy family, it was odd, in a way, that I became interested in fighting. I never saw much of it, growing up. In fact, it was only once I graduated from college, went out on my own, and lived in a few cities that I started to see some real violence, and this deeply changed how I thought about it. After that, seeing a few street fights, hearing my neighbor abusing his girlfriend, I could never see fighting in a romantic light any more. Seeing a fight in a Kung fu movie is one thing, and I love a good Kung fu flick, but seeing it in real time and in real life, feeling the toxic energy of it, the emotional intensity of it, is something else.

It was odd that I became interested in martial arts, but then, my interests have always been intense, and usually odd. I fell in love with playing guitar for ten years, and played every day. I went through a magick/occult phase in high school. I wrote poetry every day for a while, mostly in college. I also went through a Tai Chi/qigong phase. My interests tend toward obsession. In that way, martial arts made some sense, and again, I wanted, on some level, and this wasn't that unconscious at the time either, some kind of initiation into being a man. Part of this includes doing scary things, like sparring.

Another angle was that I was, from a pretty early age, very heady, very intellectual. I was not into sports. Gym classes were, for me, some of the most embarrassing and anxiety producing moments. I hated my gym teacher in elementary and middle school, and some other later ones, for a long time, and not because they were such bad folks, but because I was naturally clumsy, physically awkward, and didn't gravitate toward sports. I think people need various kinds of balance. Is does not mean that everyone has to work out a lot, or become athletes, but being all in the head, or all in the body can make you unbalanced. I was up in the head, so I resented my teachers because I blamed them for putting me in situations where I was awkward and uncomfortable.

I took acid for the first time in High School. I used other drugs too, but the psychedelics were the ones I was really interested in, having read some of Terence McKenna's books in middle school. His descriptions of "machine elves" fascinated me, and he seemed like such a smart guy. Carlos Castenada was another one. My parents did not forbid from reading this stuff. They were a little wary, maybe, but I knew they'd "experimented," and their policy on the stuff was something like, be careful, and do it at home if you have to, so you're safe.

I wanted to do psychedelics, and could only find weed, until late in High School, which was okay, in some ways, I was a very enthusiastic pothead. But I did acid once, freshman year, which was fake, and then got the real thing junior year, I think. In college, these things were easily found, if you wanted them, and I did acid maybe ten times, mushrooms, thirty or forty, all told. But going back to the discussion of being up in the head- I wanted some kind of magical, shamanistic, transformative experience through drugs, like I read about in McKenna, and Castenada, and I did, on a few occasions, get some small version of that, but I also started experiencing some physical problems. At some point, in High School, I developed some real anxiety, what you might call social anxiety, getting very nervous just being around other people, and tending to shut down, and also some balance problems, and difficulty walking.

The balance problems weren't terrible, it wasn't like I'd fall over when I was going around, but i started to feel very awkward about the process of walking, when I went out. My ankles felt too flexible, and I developed a habit of looking down a lot, as I walked, both out of some anxiety about being seen, and looking at other people, but also just to see where my feet were going. Somehow, mysteriously, I lost the intuitive sense most people have of where to put their feet, which cracks to step over, where to move your balance as you go forward on sidewalk, grass, blacktop. So I developed a habit of looking down, stooping over, to see where to put my feet, and it became a very conscious, awkward process.

You can imagine that, along with anxiety and discomfort socializing with people, this altogether made going out of the house really painful, which, in turn, produced shame, shame that I couldn't even do something as simple as walk around in public.

The discussion of the values and dangers of psychedelics, or drugs in general, is a vast one, and one that I'm not trying to make in any complete sense here. One thing, however, about psychedelics, and I have some experience in this area, is that they can make you reevaluate even the smallest, most mundane aspects of life. Things which have become rote, and unconscious, like talking to a cashier or walking past someone on a sidewalk, can become alien. It's like you're evaluating these strings of actions from the perspective of an alien, or someone who has never done them before. Picking up a glass of water, making a noise with your throat, these become new, confusing, shocking things, sometimes. And this feeling of a focal shift, and evaluating from some blank outside point of view, can often bleed over into your life after the trip. This is one of the promises and dangers of tripping. If you gain some kind of real insight from a trip, that can stay with you after, for a while. If you feel panicky, or experience some kind of horror, as many psychedelics voyagers do, that will also tend to stay with you. For someone who hasn't done these things at all, think of the latter like a car crash. The intensity of it, the adrenaline, all the emotions that come up, don't disappear the next day, they continue to influence you well into the future, and that very intensity seems to burn the experience more deeply into your psyche. I can't, in all fairness, say that no one should do drugs, for many reasons, my own history being one, but with stronger psychedelics, the after effects must be a consideration.

For mysterious reasons, but drugs being one, I'm sure, my body seemed to fall apart. At that age, I was aware of the traditional stories of shamans in training having near death experiences, or experiences of their bodies being disassembled, and then reassembled, and I thought of these as analogous to my condition. At the same time, I was just suffering greatly. I can't say that the shamanic initiation, or imitation, idea was just a matter of wishful thinking, and I can't say that the mental instability and suffering were the whole story either. It was both, as is so often the case.

My body seemed to fall apart. Doing simple things, like greeting people, making eye contact, especially walking, became nightmarish adventures in discomfort. Around this time, I got interested in Kung fu, then Aikido, then Tai Chi. Although I'd done sports, unwillingly and badly, since I was young, I actually wanted to become more graceful, coordinated, develop some power in my body. Up until that point, I had spent so much time reading, doing art, talking to people, doing things in my head. Largely through a series of mistakes and blunders, I ended up getting back in touch with my body. (And I apologize for having talked about this before, in terms of balance; I bring it up now in a different context, so I hope that makes the repetition more or less forgivable.) It was like, in one sense, I went so far into my own mind that my body demanded some attention. Over the course of many years, I very slowly became more at home in my body. I spent hours doing forms, training with teachers and partners, doing strengthening exercises, and didn't really get all that good, but did become more in tune with my physical self, and gradually more able to walk around. I worked through the physical and psychological stuff that had made walking around outside so terrifying, from simple coordination, to posture, to distancing, to working with my own anxiety, and my ability to respond to environments in a spontaneous way. All that to be able to just be out in the world, a somewhat normal person.

I've thought many many times that, for someone like me, who has gone through a minor struggle to become more at home in the world and get over some fears, it must seem sort of strange to present a self help book. In other words, I'm not presenting this book from the perspective of someone who has struggled, and then found maturity and great financial, or artistic success. I can hold down a job now, mostly. I can maintain a relationship, pretty much. I can say that I'm more content and sane than I have been in many years. I wouldn't be writing is if I didn't think I was in a place where I could say anything at all, and have it mean something, but I know it's a little strange for someone like me, who has a menial job, who struggles to find students for classes, who is not that much more mature than everyone else, to take on the position of teacher, and take on the task of writing self help. I feel like other self help type authors do their thing from a place of some success, and my only real success is developing some degree of sanity, and a practice.

Doing Kung fu was my first real foray into practice, and from there, I was able to eventually learn to meditate. Throughout this process, coming down to earth, connecting back to my body, was a very big part of learning the path. One paradox, for me, and for everyone who has undergone difficult times, is that I would not have learned as much if I hadn't gone through the fire. I would not have connected my body and mind if I hadn't torn them apart. On the other hand, it was so hard. It is too convenient to say, "I wouldn't change a thing, it all led me to where I am today." The process was a torment, painful beyond belief, and it being mostly self-inflicted just makes it worse, because I am responsible for it. In addition, I don't know that, if I hadn't gone through my falling apart phase, I wouldn't have found some other, more gentle way to get back into my body. It's very possible that I would have, without all of the confusion and isolation of having to come back from those nether realms. There is no way to know, at all. I can't go back in time.

Here is the other issue. Even leaving aside the whole process of doing drugs, falling apart, putting myself back together, I had a few experiences while on drugs that I found mind opening. To quantify it, which is a little bizarre, I know, but to quantify it, maybe ten percent of the experiences were meaningful, the rest neutral or negative. I will relate one that happened when I took LSD in college.

I went to Oberlin College. It is a multifaceted place. One of those facets is an abundance of drugs, which is not unusual at a college, but spelled trouble for me, at least in my first year and a half there. I have done LSD many times, and stopped taking it when I was about twenty or twenty one. I don't think it is the worst drug in the world, certainly not comparable to something as addictive as cocaine, or heroin, and not as pervasive and problematic as alcohol. Generally, I found, the supposed spiritual insights that came up on while imbibing were fake, the kind of false insights that you might imagine a young kid coming up with if you asked them to write about what God is, or the meaning of life, and the possibility of insight or breaking through to some other level of reality were reasons that I used LSD. I am not laying out a pro versus con type discussion here, so let me just say that it's very possible to find positives about this chemical, and, again, it's not the worst. The insights were mostly artificial, though, and, to add injury to insult, there is the bad trip. I am getting to my mind opening experience at college, but just before that, a little tangent.

The bad trip is something no one can understand unless they've had it. I would never have been able to imagine it before having tried psychedelics. You can see bad trips portrayed in movies and TV, often as a joke or a dig at hippies, but any kind of teasing or mocking portrayal of a bad trip underplays the horror of it. When you take any psychedelic, including weed, your mind and its movements become magnified, amplified, and your normal coping mechanisms for controlling thoughts, tamping down emotions, using perspective, being reasonable, tend to fall apart in the whirling, pulsing, powerful space of the drug experience. If you're preoccupied with being lonely, and you trip, you could end up with four or five hours of agonizing isolation and loneliness, worse than you'd ever imagined before. If something unpleasant happens, the trip could go from nice to horrific in an instant. The following story actually preceded one of these trips.

But I'm not trying to tell that story here, just the moments that preceded it. Of course, even if the night was mentally unpleasant for me, I did get over it. If I remember correctly, this happened in the Fall. I took the acid, and sat in my friend Dave's room with some others, waiting for it to kick in. After some time, I started to feel it, and by that point in my life, I was familiar with that feeling. I can feel it a tiny bit now just by thinking about it, a rush of energy and intensity, a visual change, and some vague feeling of something momentous about to happen. I used to have a pair of blue silky pants made out of some kind of polyester. I was wearing those, I'd gotten them from a friend in High School, and had somehow come to the conclusion that they looked cool, so I was wearing them around on a regular basis. As I felt the drug seep into my mind and body, I was looking around, probably, at my hands, probably, because for some reason your hands become utterly fascinating to watch when your tripping, and my blue shiny pants.

239

Selfless Self Help

I watched the folds and waves of blue fabric morph and melt, and I tried to explain to my friends what was happening. (I'm sure they knew what was happening anyway without my having to give a play by play description.) For some reason, as I observed my mind forming concepts and words, to go along with my fantastic visual perception of the undulating silky pants, the moment I tried to express those words to others, they fell short, and the perception had changed. The falling short and the constant changes seemed to dovetail or happen simultaneously (and to say this doesn't give the magical, entrancing, maddeningly inexpressible quality of it). Things were changing so fast, and words or ideas were unable to come close enough to capturing them, plus, that gap of precision was widened by the changing quality of what I saw.

To this day, I hold this memory up as a real insight into the way things work. Life, and our perceptions, do constantly change. Words never quite get to the heart of things. This missing the point quality of words is exacerbated by the fact of change. Now, as we move into the "mind" section of the book, where language is so important, remember this. The basic, fundamental insight into language happens in terms of change, the always missing the mark way of language (based on how things are change). I had a real insight at that moment, the same kind which can be discovered through meditation and various practices. However, drugs proved to be more harmful than meditation, and less reliable. On that very night, in reality, the rest of my trip proved to be painful.

My drug adventuring phase was difficult, self inflicted and messy. I don't think I'd do it the same way again, given that imaginary choice. But every now and then, something of valuable did emerge from it, from the drugs. Those years were an initiation for me, the first of many. I found my way out of the drug world, and found a way to come back to my body, out of the clouds of abstracted intellect, which is where psychedelics tend to be, anyway. Things really fell apart, and personally, putting them back together has been the most important point. To write this off as a mere recovery process would be too pragmatic. To elevate those years of struggle to just some kind of awakening or shadow shamanic invitation would be arrogant. It was both.

The final section of this book will be the least down to earth, the least practical. It is not about habituation, or loosening the tight belt of hypocrisy and judgement; it is about spiritual experience, the living experience of the "sacred world," alive, pulsing with energies, flush with meaning. If you have been with me so far, I suspect you'll stay the rest of the way, but I would understand fully

241

Selfless Self Help

if you don't, because this part of the trip is stranger, wilder, less a

laboratory of wisdom, and more a forest.

The Next Step on This Perilous Journey of Reading

Human beings understand too much. Seung Sahn

What I will do for the rest of this book is write a little more about Trungpa and Pema, go some more into the Tarthang Tulku TSK material, and present a series of Selfless Self Help slogans I developed. There are ten right now, but I imagine that number will get larger over time. The first one is, "you can't jump over yourself." I have not shared every embarrassing detail of my struggle with drugs and my process of putting my life together, but you have an idea of what I went through, and just by how long it took, how hard it was. For anyone who wants to improve, to get past limitations, or process whatever festering neurosis lurk in the mind, the impulse can be to push forward, and when things take years, or decades, it gets frustrating. I wish every day that I was more mature, more together, that the work I've done could have borne fruit much faster, but that's the nature of this path. It is gradual. I remember, on a road trip with some college friends, staying at the house of an acquaintance who had just had some supposed breakthrough on mushrooms or acid, him telling us over and over about how he had figured it all out. When I asked him, I think it was me, or maybe a friend, to explain his vision, he just said some things about the Tao te Ching, perhaps mixed in with some other less traditional spiritual stuff, basically a garbage pile of fake insight. I mean, at one point, he was literally saying, "I've figured it out," it being everything. As soon as someone says that they've figured it all out, you know they're pretty lost. This has little to do with whether you've taken exotic drugs, or not. It happens that millions of very normal, hardworking people also think they've got it all figured out. Both sets are wrong. Like Korean Zen master Seung Sahn said, people understand too much. Not knowing is a better bet, and a more exciting journey anyway.

This is a gradual path. You don't usually figure it all out. To put it another way, those moments of figuring it all out come up continually, but are relative moments of figuring it all out, against a background of a larger progression. Over time, I think that the repetitive nature of those "now I know" moments makes it easier to understand that you don't know. Straining for some fast breakthrough, or thinking you know, is jumping over yourself. Just like being grossed out by the psychological mess you are leads to wanting to jump over yourself.

This slogan is especially relevant to meditation practice. When you sit, or walk, just do the practice as you understand it, and as you've been taught. You don't need to create a special experience or force some calm state of mind. This point is more important when you start out as a mediator, but I think it holds some truth all the way along the path. The practices, and I'm speaking here as a Buddhist, but I'm sure this is true of a lot of other traditions also, are set up so that they build over time- over minutes and hours, and over years. This means that you cannot achieve incredible bliss and centeredness in a ten minute session. Good to do a ten minute session, I just did slightly less than that myself, before writing this, but the fantasy of meditating a little tiny bit, and forcing a change of state is just that, fantasy. Don't jump over yourself.

Not jumping over means facing yourself. A big reason it is tempting to try to attain some kind of bliss or insight too quickly, or try to numb or quiet the mind, when we sit, is that it can be so embarrassing to look at yourself. It so embarrassing that we don't even want to talk about how embarrassing it is. It's that humiliating. We can't look at our own face because we want to save face. The problem comes when you realize that whatever you run from seems to find you, humming in the background. Silence seems to hold this power, is energy, and it is 110% important to relate with silence. The words, the language work in terms of silence. They mix with silence, and also, they are silence. My insight and my development are not yet great, but this is about as far as they go. Because I generally identity silence with space, which is not the only way to see it, but makes a certain sense, we're talking also about space and language- language in space, language as space.

This goes back to my story of the blue pants. The language, as it developed, became spacious in a way that was beguiling. Our job, as practitioners, is in many ways to see that as clearly as possible, the spacelike qualities in and around language, and then to make choices based on that reality. This is perceptual reality, so when I say "language," one thing I mean is perceptions themselves. Look at a tree, a building, your own face. See how they interact with the air about them, and shift, if you can. This is a language of sorts, as are all perceptions. One teacher, when talking about this, the "vividness of perceptions," ('vivid' coming from the French *vivre*, to live, a living quality or presence) said that this will increase as we move along the path, and it will not always be easy. Sometimes, she said, we will be cut open in these moments of connecting, through sense, with the world, but this is a good thing.

Karlins

It means that we were really there, we were really, as she said, available.

Selfless Self Help

From the Old World to the New World

"The warrior is constantly reminded that he has to be on the spot, on the dot, because he is choosing to live in a world that does not give him the setting sun's concept of rest." Trungpa

I used to hate vacations, and I'm still not great at them (although, since leaving school, I don't have as many as I used to). I would spend weeks looking forward to time off. I wouldn't have homework, for a while, and I could see friends, spend time alone, stay up late, do whatever I wanted. The problem was, I would look forward to vacations, and then, once they arrived, I wouldn't know what to do. TV got boring quickly, even if you could appreciate daytime talk shows, and bad reruns. Smoking pot, when that was something I indulged in, lost its charm once the paranoia set in, or once you got tired. I might imagine projects, like writing or art, would fill the time, but often I could not find the motivation or interest once time opened up. It's a strange thing, how inspiration seems to strike when you don't have the chance to create. I've had a lot of good creative ideas at work, and it's not that I couldn't write them down and flesh them out later, but the bigger problem seems to me to be that the spark of inspiration is not there. Then again,

248

maybe I'm placing too much important on that spark. It's important, but not necessary for creation. I don't usually feel it before I get going on something.

But to get back to vacations, I used to hate them (along with birthdays and holidays, which, thankfully, now, I don't mind, even enjoy). This is the "setting sun" concept, or a version of it- that when you can do what you want, totally relax, that you will be happy, somehow things will fall into place. It doesn't usually work that way. I could see, if you're totally, one hundred percent overworked, exhausted, that a vacation might be a different story. I've never been in that position, not yet. Even then, I don't know that the total-couch potato type vacation would keep its charm past a day or two. Setting sun means that you can wallow in habitual patterns, climbing deeper into your personal cocoon. Having become a practitioner, this no longer holds its charm. At a definite point, you cross some line and those kind of things no longer appeal. You might have some small voice in the back of your head that whispers suggestions about the setting sun, still, but the part of you that's not buying it gets stronger. Truthfully, this is mostly a matter of facing facts. It's not that I used to love vacations, and then I became a meditator, and I started to work harder and get my act together. It's that I never really liked the setting sun, but I would not admit it. Another example: good friends are great, but I used to spend a lot of time, in different places where I lived, hanging out with people I didn't like that much, having conversations I found boring, draining, a waste of my energy. I felt that it was what I was supposed to do, to be social, to have a social life. I resultantly wasted a lot of time and energy on things I didn't care about. This is the setting sun, too.

The slogan "Sanity for oneself and others," is partly about this. There is an insanity to the way people live in denial of what actually satisfies them, denial of what a good life actually is. I used the term, in a talk I gave last week, that I came up with on the spot, "bizarre innocence," to refer to the way people allow themselves to be surprised at annoying things that happen over and over. Maybe you have an argument with a loved one that repeats and repeats, and yet, part of the annoyance is that you feel a little surprised when it comes up again. That's bizarre innocence, you shouldn't be so surprised. The way people live in the setting sun world has a bizarre innocence to it as well. No one is really happy in that world, but try to get them to move out! It's not easy.

You have to remember that the new world, what is known as sacred world, is an exciting place (not an escape, or a very easy place all the time, but an exciting place). Maybe exciting is the wrong word, I don't know. It's not like roller coaster type excitement. It is beautiful, and very interesting, and a lot more real than the setting sun. It is there to be enjoyed, in the form of beautiful skies, strange sounds, marvelous tastes, complex feelings in the body. It is a world where magic and celebration are real, true, as opposed to the crazy and stressful holidays of the setting sun. When you can celebrate life, and have a good time, without being neurotic or habitual, things get really good. Meditation and other such practices can seem very dour sometimes, but they have to exist in a context of celebration. If your own celebrations have seemed unpleasant or depressing up to this point, that just supports what I am saying. The setting sun is so powerful these days, in the West, but somehow, its power tends to automatically short circuit. Think about this if you go on vacation.

I'd like to emphasize holiday celebrations (even parties, if you like parties) in lieu of the vacation discussion. I have actually taught classes on this, called "Sanity for the Holidays." I have not perfected my curriculum for those classes, but it's only been two years running, at this point in time. Not only did I have trouble with vacations and birthdays, but holidays, too, in my family, were mostly difficult for me to enjoy. They didn't feel right, for some reason. Two reasons were a lack of appreciation, on my part, which is easy enough to cultivate, and a lack of understanding of the sacred. It will probably sound crazy but, truly, one big reward I enjoyed from a few years of serious practice and study were that I could enjoy holidays again. I didn't just feel depressed during them. I knew when to spend time with family, and when to take a moment or two, to get my head together (so that I didn't feel overwhelmed or end up feel I really upset later, a matter of catching my emotions before they were really off the tracks). Enjoying life is probably a good idea. You should enjoy life. This includes your own personal interpretations of birthdays, holidays, and so forth.

Enjoyment has something to do with atmosphere, at least what we're calling enjoyment in the holy context of living as a meditator. Right now, in that vein, I'm going to clean my house a little, improve the atmosphere, and see what happens, enjoyment-wise.

Coordination on Different Levels

"One thousand years of nonmovement, one thousand years of flying through space." Selfless Self Help Slogan

This one is about becoming better at both stillness and movement. That's a very simple goal, or two simple goals, and something you can work on during your day. Meditation is, on one level, about stillness. It's about stillness of the body. It leads to states where the mind becomes more still, especially in terms of the habitual discursiveness that we experience as thinking, the chattiness of the mind. The movement and stillness of the body, as you walk at work, on the street, and so on, is important too, and becoming gradually more coordinated. I'm not talking about "peak performance," or some high level of athleticism, although I envy people who can do that. I'm talking about what Trungpa called "synchronizing mind and body." One part of this is becoming more physically coordinated, in other words, less clumsy. I can say without a doubt that you don't know how to get more in synch until you start to see how clumsy you've been. This has been my experience, and having food service jobs, physical work, has

253

helped me with this. Try being clumsy as a dishwasher, or a prep cook, or working with a couple other people in a small kitchen, cleaning and dusting. You are very quickly made aware of your own clumsiness, and rewarded for not being so clumsy.

Ever since meditation and Eastern spiritual training exploded in popularity in the sixties and seventies, physical training (yoga, martial arts, energy work) have been a part of many practitioner's discipline (and discipline might suggest a solemnity that's only partly accurate- these things are fun, too, and that's part of the idea). I personally believe that, for most people, sitting meditation is a deeper way to work on the soul than these other paths, but they can complement each other. I would just suggest leaning more in the direction of sitting, than other practices, in terms of time and devotion. There are those who'd strongly disagree with this bias, and it is a bias (but one I also believe).

"One thousand years..." suggests that you should get used to the idea of putting a lot of work into both becoming more still, and becoming better at moving. The depths and heights of movement and nonmovement are good to work at and find out about. Then, there are other kinds of coordination. There's coordination in a group, or in a relationship. There's also coordination when it comes

254

to the seasons and the natural world, and this is where sacred world comes back into focus. I have found it both useful and very enjoyable to use a Tibetan calendar over the last couple of years, which is a lunar calendar. I am still learning how to use this calendar; I am still very much a novice.

The reason I started using the calendar is that I wanted to connect my practice more with the cycles of the natural world. Trungpa introduced the idea "lha, nyen and lu," in Shambhala, which previously, I think had only referred to three classes of spirits or deities. According to the Shambhala explanation, lha, nyen and lu are a way of describing everything: beginning, middle and end, Winter, Spring, Fall, parts of the body, and more. These these things are a way of categorizing reality, which one thing spirituality does, and a set of correspondences (this goes along with that). I began using a calendar because I wanted my practice to connect to this natural cycle, as described in lha, nyen, and lu, and calendars give a concrete way to do this. The seasons change, and we feel different. Some of this can be explained scientifically. We feel like staying inside when it is cold, of course, and when it warms up, everyone is excited to get out again, and enjoy the world. If you pay attention to the feelings you have, I think, you'll see that the internal experience, emotionally and energetically, of the changes of the year, is something a little more complicated than just, "it's cold, I want to stay in the house," and "it's warm, let's go out!" There are ranges of subtle feeling that arise along with the shifts in the natural world, which is the same thing as the world, and which we never totally disconnect from. Practicing meditation has put me in touch with these things slightly more than before. I can feel the change in temperatures more accurately now, the way, in the cold seasons, the earth seems to draw heat out of my body. The air can feel so many different ways against my face- crisp, bitter, slimy, a baking radiation. Yes, these examples do fit with science, but there are some sensations that are personal that do not, I think. This is very intuitive, but also common sense. Someone who writes off the subtleties of feeling would not be able to accept these ideas. To me, these are evidence that the cycle of the year has power and energy to it beyond the more commonplace alterations of temperature and precipitation. Practicing with a calendar was based on some acceptance of this idea, in line with lha, nyen, and lu, but my understanding and acceptance of this also deepened once I had been using yearly changes as a guide.

Selfless Self Help has a curriculum with a progression to it. When I teach it as a class over nine sessions, I like to start with the body scan, then contemplative meditation, and then third kind, a more relaxed meditation. These fit with lha, nyen, and lu, and the Buddhist concepts of body, speech, and mind. I also coordinate these techniques with times of year, although there is some flexibility to this. Beyond that first class, the curriculum involves meditating outside, which helps people integrate their sitting practice with work, family life, traveling around. This is essential. Meditation is never just a way to unwind and get your head together. It is something to do all the time, a method of focusing and refining the mind's energy in all situations, pleasant, plain, or unpleasant. There are no bad circumstances for practice, when it comes to meditating with daily life. There are no profane circumstances, only sacred ones. Meditation does not exactly create the sacredness, but it does make it more apparent, and it can do interesting things, where the sacredness tends to pop up or intensify.

Past that level, there is a cycle of practices based firmly on the cycles of the year. For me, as a Tibetan Buddhist, there are complexities to this that come from Buddhist theory. For instance, on full and new moons, there a variety of meditations which would be appropriate, and Vajrayana (Tibetan) Buddhists have their ways of doing these, while Theravada and Zen Buddhists have their own ways. Some other Buddhist traditions, those outside my area of knowledge, probably do it their own way, or choose to ignore, more or less, these cycles. Obviously, that's partly a matter of tradition and partly a personal choice, for the meditator. Because SSH is ecumenical, I am convinced that Christians, for instance, could find their own ways to follow a similar calendar. Granted, most Christians already have a well-established liturgical calendar, but I don't know that it would hurt to work in the ideas I'm talking about, at least for some people. There are people who'd call what I'm doing paganism, or worse, and they are not my target audience (although they're perfectly welcome too).

To give a brief sketch of what this cycle looks like, first, remember that the year, in this calendar, is broken down into three seasons (lha, nyen, and lu). Nyen combines Spring and Summer. Lu is Fall, but actually covers late Summer as well, practically speaking. Each season covers four months, and does not map with either Western or Tibetan calendars, although I am fairly satisfied with the estimated calendar I've created (in that it seems to fit pretty well with seasonal changes). Vajrayana Buddhism is well known for its deity yoga practices, which usually entail visualizations and the use of mantras. These practices are not beginner practices, but can be done without too much finagling by anyone within driving distance of a meditation center/major city. I would rather not go

258

into detail about any more specifics of the deity yogas I use with this system. It is nothing controversial or weird, but pretty simple, I just don't want people to jump into it without the right preparation or training.

I will be the first to admit that this system could be arbitrary. I think that, in a poetic sense, a sense of association or metaphor, these deity practices make some sense with the three seasons, but that doesn't mean they fit exactly, in some deeper way. I am doing this partly as an experiment. I said this in a free public talk I gave last week. I think that, even if the seasonal model does not make some kind of deeper sense, it is, first of all, not harmful, and second, a way to ensure that certain practices do get done. By saying, "do this for four months," or "do this for a month," it helps the meditator do a number of practices and get some experience in them. I have been doing this myself for a little while, and have found this pragmatic side of the calendar works pretty well. I don't jump around too much from practice to practice, but I still enjoy the variety, and get to get a taste of the energy of a number of practices. Assuming I keep going with this, the calendar will evolve and become more sophisticated. When I say that this system is ecumenical, I'm serious about this, too. I think it would be very interesting, exciting, even, for groups of Christians to get together throughout the year, and practice together based on the cycles of the natural world. The same for Muslims, Hindus, and Jews. The outer practices, the work on habits, the work on compassion, and the four basic techniques, are very open to people regardless of their faith. The inner practices, such as the deity yogas I mentioned, are generally more limited to people of one tradition or another. It is not that a Hindu, for instance, would be barred from learning how to do Chenrezig, but more like that Hindu would probably want to focus on their own traditions deity practices.

I've talked about a simple practitioner's calendar, and about the internal experience of natural cycles. One is abstract, the other very concrete. Both are examples of how sacred world moves, lives, and breathes. It is good that we are discussing this at this point, after, hopefully, you've been meditating regularly for a while, because these things don't make any sense unless you are meditating, unless you are, on a very regular basis, opening and clearing your mind. The beauty won't have room to get in if you don't.

The way to understand the cycle of practices, at this point, is an overall approach to connecting with the moving energies of the natural world. I see this as something people can work on after having learned the basics of sitting, which is traditional, and is what I did.

Selfless Self Help

Breath, that Mysterious Substance, and the Rhythm of Time

When we pause, allow a gap and breathe deeply, we can experience instant refreshment. Suddenly, we slow down, and there's the world. Pema Chodron

Up to this point, I have not talked about the breath so much, partly due to the fact that the meditation exercises I tend to use in Selfless Self Help are not breath based (at least not directly) and partly because I am avoiding talking much about meditation at all. It is such an oral tradition, a practice that must be transmitted in person, not in a book. Still, many people do use the breath to meditate, and I include it as part of the contemplative technique. It's fascinating that, as I've experienced being a student, most teachers, even those who rely on using the breath for meditation very heavily, don't talk much about it either. You'll often read people writing about the traditional uses of the terms for breath, like prana, and how here have been many cultures that subscribe to ideas about breath, energy, spirit and so forth, being deeply connected, and this is done, usually, as kind of argument by implication, and an argument based on tradition; the breath is a valid tool because many cultures have implied or spelled out that breath is powerful and somewhat magical, and the breath is a valid tool because there is such a strong history across cultures of using this one thing. Maybe those ancient traditions were wrong about a lot, but they must've gotten some things right, especially if there's some kind of overlap or consensus.

I don't totally disagree here. But I do think that the best argument for the breath as a key is experiential, and this is probably why so many teachers don't talk a lot about it. It is best just experienced. This works well when you've been practicing regularly for a while, and breath practice has become more or less natural.

The quote from Ani Pema speaks to the simplicity and power of using the breath. Much of life gets swept away by doing stuff, and doing stuff is amazing. We all want satisfying accomplishments and fun and creativity, but the momentum and feelings of action easily destroy our ability to use the mind and body skillfully, gracefully, so using some technique, such as the breath, is important to regain skillfulness. Once regained, taking action can become more balanced, and the striving for accomplishment, fun, and creativity can come back into focus. We need a technique, or a "crutch" as Trungpa liked to call it, in order to be more present. It is possible to just be present, and use this as a kind of technique, but sometimes this is not easy or not enough, or we are not well trained enough. It's hard to spend a lot of time "on the cushion" or "on the mat," especially when retreats and workshops often mean unpaid time off of work. It is conceivable that you and I can get better at practicing, even if longer retreats and more time sitting are not in the cards at the moment, and meditating in the midst of daily life is a big part of this. There are two main ways to do this.

The first is to include some formal practice in one's day. I used to take the subway to work every morning. I didn't have a car, and was glad not to. Many times I would sit, close my eyes, and practice the body scan technique, and I found it worked amazing well, especially if I could sit for thirty or forty minutes at a time. I made sure that I felt comfortable enough with the people around me, and would open my eyes, usually, whenever people got on or off the train, to make sure I didn't feel threatened at all, sitting with eyes closed. I don't think I ever had an issue with being bothered, or even someone who I felt really worried about, although maybe once or twice I just decided not to meditate that time, or until they got off. Overall, my experience of New Yorkers was that they were kind, open, and very helpful. I thought, too, at the time, that most could tell what I was doing, when I would practice. You can tell when someone is practicing by their presence.

There are many ways to work formal practice into your day, and the biggest challenge is figuring out how to make it work with your schedule, and your environment. In some places, finding a quiet place to sit won't be a problem. In a big city, even reciting a mantra out loud might not get a single raised eyebrow; certainly New Yorkers are famous for being used to strange behavior. In other places, you will face more scrutiny and less accepting attitudes, and doing more subtle forms of practice may be advisable, depending on how much you care about the reactions of others. This is a tricky point, and one everyone has to engage individually: how much are we, as yogis, trying to blend in, and how much are we trying to stand out? How much are we trying to be average folks, and how much are we working on just being ourselves and not caring at all about the judgments of others?

These are things I think all meditators have to grapple with on their own, and consider in light of who they are, their tradition, and their own growth. I'm not suggesting we all start sitting in lotus position on park benches, but I'm not totally against it either. It's mostly personal, and based on situations.

Selfless Self Help

The second way is to work informal practice into life.

Contemplating things like habits and hypocrisy are ways to do this.

Coming back to the breath is another way, as Pema reminds us.

There is a slogan in SSH, "catch your breath," that's about this. The

way it feels when you've been rushing about, or distracted, and

then you breathe, and the present moment arises more fully around

you, this is an example of catching the breath. It's not really about

catching it and then making yourself breathe deeply for the rest of

the day, but more like touching in with the breath, and then going

back to what you were doing, whether it's ordering coffee,

counting change, or parking. There is a pause before the breath

gets caught, I think, just like Pema was talking about, and that

seems to be important. The pause somehow creates both the space

and groundedness to feel and become one with the breath again.

Catching the breath is also something to experience in a meditation

session. Many techniques work both during formal and informal

practice sessions. They cross over, and thank goodness, because

this allows us to integrate the spiritual and supposedly non-

spiritual parts of our lives.

Tarthang Tulku talks about the rhythm of time, and what he calls

"decision points," and catching the breath is an example of this.

Remember the Pema quote about the gap and the world

reappearing. I have been contrasting the intensity of doing what we all do, doing stuff, and that moment of coming back, through using the key of the breath as a felt sensation (not an idea of the breath). The idea of time's rhythm connects: there is definitely a rhythm at play when we get caught by housework, or using a computer, or talking. Now that rhythm is, in a way, just a bunch of things happening in sequence, how else could they happen? Then again, think about it. All periods of activity have some feeling to them, and this is common sense, even if science has not caught up, in this case, to common sense. During holiday preparations, things can feel hectic and pressured. Things feel similar when I rush to get my shit together in the morning before driving to work. Time spent alone, with no plan, can feel slow, lonely, barren, too quiet or empty. Walking through a forested park in the summer, with many bird calls around, lush vegetation, the crunching and crackling of footsteps, smells of earth and rotting play matter, has a rhythm and feeling to it. Sacred world is related to recognizing, and before even that, accepting that these rhythms and associated feeling tones, have some reality. Yes, it is possible to categorize those feelings and the concepts of rhythm as personal associations or interpretations that are merely our own. How many times, though, have you had a crazy stressful day, and told this to someone else, to get "yes, me too" as a response? Think about the opposite, when you've shared delightful moments with someone who has seen the same rhythm as you, those times when you seem to share thoughts or have the same idea at the same time?

I won't say something here like "it's all part of a plan" or something vaguely explanatory like that, but I do believe, based on some study and experience, that things in life have rhythms (think back to the chapter on seasons and synchronizing mind and body) and that those rhythms can't be written as merely subjective experience. Subjective experience is a funny thing. It seems to extend beyond one subject. The breath is a key that opens the door to the senses, and the worlds of the senses. Sacredness is not far off, even if it is easy to forget about it, or conceptualize it into vague dreaminess. This key also interlocks with time, and what Tarthang calls decision points.

Each 'point of decision is the emerging gathering of *all known knowledge*, at whatever level it operates. In the gathered wholeness of the 'point of decision', nothing is left out, and choice is freely available. The known world is sustained from moment to moment on the basis of ever-emerging 'points of decision'.

"*In this ongoing 'emergency', all that is is invariably at stake.* Since this is so, what binds us 'now' is evanescent- freedom can be 'recovered' at any moment.

268

Karlins

"The chain of 'decision points' duplicates itself, interweaving time and knowledge. But the chain is always forming anew- at each point in the chain we choose to maintain what is. Though the choice we make is based on the sum of our knowledge, it grows also out of the rhythm of time, for choosing is action, and action responds to and is powered by the temporal dynamic... We can restore the underlying balance. We can recover the true significance of 'points of decision' as points that gather the whole of being and return to a freedom of always emerging creativity. (Tarthang Tulku) (All italics by author)

I love the sense of intensity and urgency the italics give here, along the meaning implied by the use of quotation marks, which is a hallmark of the TSK style of presentation. I don't think I can do justice to this excerpt fully, even if I were to spend hundreds of pages on it, but let me draw out a few points. This quote comes at the end of a chapter which starts with talk about the tension between the "wholly open realm of creativity," in other words, being in sacred space, realized activity, and "conventional reality." This is what I've been talking about with doing and the coming back to the breath. It's the big problem, in a way, how to get from being entangled in confusion to being able to act creatively in the moment.

One idea Tarthang brings up is that points of decision are not just chances to do something interesting, but also the culmination of all knowledge. Literally, all time and knowledge have built up to this point here. All ideas, plans, systems of thought existing here and now, are based on their predecessors and influences. History means that everything connects and goes back to an initial point of beginning, or back just forever, if there is no initial beginning point. In either case, it's a long long time, and any point in time, where actions happen, is connected to all other points. If this seems exciting to you in some way, or invigorating, it does for me too, it should. The cocoon mindset forgets this, the moment as an intensification of all points, but that forgetting is not helping anybody. Thinking and study can help you remember, and the breath can help you remember too. There are layers of interesting power to the breath. I highly recommend that you experiment with using the breath in all sorts of real life situations. I have done this myself and found it very interesting, very useful. Both in-breath and out-breath can have differing feelings, differing results when used in real life situations.

Freedom can be recovered. It can be uncovered. The breath is a good way to do this. It can take you from knowing too easily what is going on, in the way you'd give some story about who you are to an acquaintance or someone interviewing you for a job, to don't know mind. That mind is friends with the temporal dynamic, the dance of time and space.

Ideas get spacious naturally, heavenly, up in the sky. Everyone is a philosopher. The best thing about the breath is probably that it is hard to bullshit. It brings you back down to earth, which is sacred, waiting to greet you. As ideas become too spacious, language takes on certain shapes. If you've seen a friend or loved one thinking obsessively, worrying, or lost in thought about something, you know this is one kind of spaciousness of thought. The words in their head are taking on a kind of form as they space out. These are times when you might try to draw someone out, or bring them back, or engage with them. All of those interpersonal considerations aside, think of this kind of moment of spaciness as an example of language. What happens when you connect to the breath, catch the breath, in those moments? We have probably all heard famous teachers' exhortations to, when the rhythm of time gets choppy (stress) or busy, come back to the breath. This is great, no arguments here. To add to that, however, what can we do with breath, beyond just becoming more grounded, on those occasions of stressful energy? When the language of our world can be heard, we can use breath, tune into breath, for a multitude of purposes.

Power of Language

The next slogan goes, "Don't get lost in words." This one is interesting to me because it doesn't mean that words are utterly meaningless, or that they're the answer to everything either. It means that whatever power words might have, they are easy to get lost in, and this is something to watch out for.

As quite a few meditation teachers have pointed out, when people start, they will often complain that they were "thinking a lot," because sitting and following the breath, or counting breaths, or scanning the body, somehow allows us to hear our thoughts in a way we don't normally. People tend to ignore their thoughts. People tend to ignore themselves, in some ways. When newcomers start the practice of meditation, they notice their thoughts more, and it seems like this is, a lot of times, an unpleasant or confusing thing to feel, the onrush of thoughts. That's actually an interesting question: why are we bothered at all by our thoughts, even by torrents of thoughts? What is it about thoughts, or the feeling of thinking, that is so difficult to handle? I really don't know. Whatever the reasons are, it is, most often, not easy or pleasant, although it can get easier over time. This is one kind of getting lost in words, because thoughts are made up partly of words.

Not getting lost is one of the purposes of practice. The whole mindfulness thing, which has become so popular in some circles, recently, could be described as not getting lost. Coming back to the present moment, and being more aware of sensations, and of thoughts as thoughts, is a very powerful and subtle way to become unlost. It is so powerful, as a matter of fact, that it's hard to separate it out from other techniques. Other techniques still have something to do with being present, and recognizing bought as they are, and so other techniques can be called forms of mindfulness.

Let me get back to words, though. The negative or lostness side of words is evident enough, I think. Just in case it's not, think about times when you've been extremely stressed, overwhelmed, depressed, or upset. In those times, words in the form of thoughts become very powerful. If your thoughts, at those instances, could somehow become clearer, if you could find your way out of that maze, the pain would most definitely decrease, at least slightly, if not completely. To add to this confusion, and possible redemption, there are the words of other people, which can have such a strong influence on us. A single word can create whole firestorms of internal reaction. This is true for you and me, and this means my own words have done this, too. "Words have no weapons," the master Shantideva wrote, "but they tear men's minds to pieces."

To take another approach, words can have strong effects without being purely toxic. If you ask someone out on a date and they say yes, that has an effect. Hearing music and understanding lyrics that speak to exactly what you're feeling has an effect. Being able to express yourself to a friend or family member and finding just the right words, in the moment, is a beautiful thing.

In maybe a verbose way I'm saying that words have power, and can be good, or bad. Obviously, they don't just fit into those two rigid categories, but you know what I mean. Here is a quote from Tarthang Tulku about words.

In the course of knowing that language invites, a label is applied to set something in place, so that what is labeled can be set aside. Knowledge is restricted to establish the appropriate references to the relevant labels. Confined within the structures that language acknowledges and authorizes, knowledge cannot really go 'beneath' language itself.

That last line, about going beneath language, is what really got me. Firstly, isn't that true? So many problems are language problems. Try to figure something out, try to solve an issue with yourself or someone else, and you're mostly dealing with words, most of the time. Because you're dealing with words, and words exist at a surface level, and come with sets of restrictive rules, those problems are very hard to solve. I can remember so many times when I've argued with my wife, my parents, and others, and I felt like easy solutions were within reach, but the workings or language itself made it so hard to get anywhere. Yes, personalities, and those dynamics are huge, but just the way language works seems to make finding any simple fix nearly impossible. That's first, the near impossibility of going beneath language with our current forms of knowledge.

Second is that we then clearly need other forms of knowledge. This is where intuition comes in. I am no big intuitive expert, but I think it is important, and has to do with listening, taking hints, and paying attention.

Just to circle back to the beginning of the quote, what Tarthang so intriguingly makes clear is that creating concepts is the path of language, which, for most of us, means the path of knowledge.

Selfless Self Help

There must be forms of knowledge beyond language, and intuition seems like it approaches this, but most times, knowing means swimming through oceans of words. Once a concept is formed, and a label created, that thing, or what we have made into a thing, is set aside. This is where not knowing, or beginner's mind, comes in. When we think we know too easily, and apply a label, that setting aside can lead to ignoring the real truths of a time and place. If I look at my phone and quickly think, "yeah, phone, I know that," I ignore the actual living experience of the phone's shape, heaviness, density, smoothness, color. I miss out on everything. I get lost in a single word.

So, knowledge then, a lot of the time, is about making connections between the labels we have already collected, in ways that are tried and true. Not that we should somehow abandon this for starry-eyed wonderment about the now, as if they would somehow solve everything and create all the knowledge we need on the spot, but that there are many many times when our knowledge falls flat, and pain results. These times, language is failing us, or we are failing language. The knowledge we are using as a tool is insufficient in those cases, chained down by words that are normative, clumsy, anxiously plain, or inaccurate. This is a place where the creativity of TSK comes in. It is a theme in the series. Different teachers paint different pictures of what it is like to become realized, or approach enlightenment. For Tarthang Tulku, creativity and caring are both, it seems, integral parts of this process. This must be different for everyone.

One thing I want to reinforce is that meditation and the meditator's life is not about purging thoughts from the mind. It's more about changing one's relationship with thoughts, from a bad one to a good one. This is delicate point, and partly because I'm using words to discuss words, which is always a trip. The delicacy is more about the growth process of a meditator, however, and based on my own limited experience, and what more experienced folks have written and said, thoughts do, as you practice year after year, change. Trungpa told Pema Chodron that it was like waves at the beach. They knock you down, but over time they get smaller. Other people say that it's like the thoughts become less substantial. They are still there, moving around, doing their thing, but they seem to have less substance to them, less weight. The Insight Meditation teacher Jack Kornfield, in his book *After the Ecstasy, the Laundry* relates an account from one longtime meditator who said that his experience of thoughts changing was like having a bunch of stuff in a small, cramped room. Over time, that room became as big as an airplane hangar. The stuff hadn't changed that much, but there was more space around it.

Not only is this life not about eliminating thoughts, which is something people do mention sometimes, this desire to throw away or get rid of thoughts, but thoughts can even be enjoyed. Not only can practice bring you more space, but it can allow you to have more fun in your thoughts, and use them more skillfully. Why wouldn't you want to enjoy the thoughts? They will probably always be there. It's like you're stuck on a desert island with them. At first, they might infuriate you, but after a while, you would learn to appreciate them, marvel even at them. Appreciate is really the word, here. I can't tell you how many times I've just let my thoughts wander, and been amazed by the strange stories and imaginings that have spiraled forth. Your thoughts are like natural television. To add to this, thinking better means that it's not just about letting go of thoughts. Sometimes, if we want to create, problem solve, or engage with something, thinking in fresh and insightful ways is just the ticket. Sometimes, the cliche of letting go of thoughts can actually be a way to avoid doing what needs to be done. Spiritual tools easily become part of the walls of the cocoon. It's just how it works. So, if you're mulling over how much you hate your job, and trying to "let it go," the real answer might be to figure out a solution! Get a new job. Find a way to make things better at your current job. In truth, letting go is important, I would venture, but it has to do be done the right way, and not as some kind of avoidance mechanism.

Tarthang wrote about the difficulty of going beneath the structures of language to find real knowledge. The blessings of meditation, however you understand them, allow people to weave higher forms of knowing in with lower, higher forms of language in with lower. There are many alternatives to the conventional way of doing things. It should be beyond clear by this point that this is one of the main messages of this book. Remember, do something different.

Not bound by language, knowledge can open to communication at a deeper level, exploring the 'logos' directly. It can maintain a subtle balance, absorbed in positions but free from positions, ready to use language in ways both new and old. Balanced in this manner, we can draw on language without being caught up in it; we can accept conventional patterns without accepting their claims. Then, each thought, each presentation, each word, and each action can become a perfect gesture of balance.

There you have it. Language is everywhere, and it is powerful. It is hard to go below the surface of, in part because of it being so pervasive. At the same time, it is not all powerful. Growing as a practitioner means having moments where listening and talking are not dominated by the positions language subtly demands, the this versus that, this based on that structure. More specifically, Tarthang writes that this level of realization, and he doesn't say that it has to be permanent or last more than a brief moment, involves balance, the use of both higher and lower knowledge, higher and lower forms of language, use of positions in a free fashion, and use of or at least understanding of conventional patterns in a free fashion. This all connects to what he calls "logos," which is extremely relevant to a discussion of language.

As someone who is not highly realized or enlightened, it is hard for me to talk from my experience about these markers, and talking from experience is what I try to do, and what I think spiritual writers have to do. Otherwise, it becomes academic, and just try reading a book about spiritual practice by a nonpracticing academic. They're just awful. They used to be the norm, and luckily, there are not anymore, or at least they're becoming much less prevalent, I think.

All that being said, let me try to say a little about this map of word use. The higher/lower discrimination is key. Tarthang includes higher/lower knowing, and language. Like all nondual systems I am aware of, TSK is faced with the challenge of talking about duality and progressions while at the same time, juggling this with the truth of nonduality and the inherent problems and inaccuracy of progressions.

Higher/Lower- First, there would have to be the existence of these categories, and then would come their use, in terms of language. In a very rough way, it's not too hard to get what this means. Higher versus lower knowing could mean more insightful and thoughtful thinking as opposed to less insightful and thoughtful thinking. There are so many shapes and colors to knowledge and insight. I just listened to a podcast yesterday that featured a doctor answering some questions about blood tests, among other things. Blood testing, for health, is not something I've done, not even something I'm that interested in right now, but hearing this man's depth of understanding and his humble thoughtfulness when addressing questions he'd received was good listening. I enjoyed it. It remained me how little I know about the science of the body, and modern approaches to health. He displayed some higher knowledge. He was not enlightened, as far as I could tell, so his higher knowledge was not the ultimate knowledge, but still, not too shabby! This fellow also demonstrated some higher use of language just based on his speaking clearly, thoughtfully, with honesty, and by being very focused, very together. Think of the opposite of all the qualities I've talked about. He wasn't unfocused, dishonest, careless, or sloppy. He wasn't uninformed about his subject. Those would be lower forms of knowledge and expression.

Now, I said something about the juggling of duality and nonduality. I have to try to clarify that a little bit. All systems purporting to explain and give some access to the divine, wherever and whoever they come from, have to address this, somehow, the tension of "relative and ultimate." We usually think about life and the universe in relative, very constricted conceptual grounds, but this is not the whole picture. The words/directness idea is a pretty decent example of this. As I sit here, at my kitchen table, with the chimes outside sounding away, and some books strewn around, along with some sage I burnt earlier, and some leftover rolls from breakfast, I usually think of this all as labels. There are "rolls" and "sage" and "chimes." I don't pay too much attention to their details, the sense data they encompass, or other subtleties, which may not even be super subtle, but I just overlook them in favor of wordy labels. It's like Tarthang wrote, labels allow us to put aside things. This is "knowing too much" as Seung Sahn put it. Don't know mind is about actually living, while assuming you know is about ignoring direct experience in favor of concepts or words.

One layer is to see that things are not their labels, and this is critical, because tasting this directness means approaching nonduality. Nonduality is the world as a living thing not utterly bound by concept. The next layer is trying to reconcile that directness, that taste of nonduality with the concepts of dualism. It is never enough to stop at the first layer and say, "ok, it is just what we experience, beyond words," because, and I think there a few reasons, tut this is a big one, the nondual experience tends to automatically become dualistic again. If just working with the label "roll" is a problem because we miss out on the real roll, with all its textures, color, shape, smell, just trying to stay on the level of dismissing words becomes its own missing out. It becomes another concept. Instead of hypnotizing ourselves with the word concept of "roll," we're hypnotizing ourselves with the concept of a person experiencing directly, or with direct experience. Would that this were not true. Sadly, the mind seems to have an instinct built in that keeps us from becoming enlightened easily, so any taste we get of the nondual state hardens fairly quickly into dualism. Our minds are clever. Like I said, I'm amazed sometimes to look at the intricate mazelike workings of my mind. The mind's ability to suddenly and quietly turn a nondual moment into a separated one is an aspect of that strength and creativity. It just happens to be an application of said strength and creativity that gets in the way of wisdom.

Tarthang has given a very good description of what it is like at the level of fruition, he level at which wisdom is not only trained, but applied to real life. In regards to the duality/nonduality issue, another very good one is the idea of what Trungpa called "basic goodness," which I wrote about briefly in the first section. I'd like to come back to that now, since it's relevant. So, again, the issue at hand is the need to deal with both the immediacy and concept-unraveling qualities of nonduality, and the pervasiveness and trickiness and importance of duality.

Earth is always earth... Likewise, sky is always sky; heaven is always heaven above you. Whether it is snowing or raining, or the sun is shining, whether it is daytime or nighttime, the sky is always there. In that sense, we know that heaven and earth are trustworthy.

The logic of basic goodness is very similar. When we speak of basic goodness, we are not talking about having allegiance to good and rejecting bad. Basic goodness is good because it is unconditional, or fundamental. It is there already, in the same way heaven and earth are there already...

The natural law and order of this world is not 'for' or 'against'. Fundamentally, there is nothing that either threatens us or promotes our point of view... We often take for granted this basic law and order in the universe, but we should think twice. (Trungpa, Shambhala)

Basic goodness is good not in the way good food is tasty and bad food is disgusting. It is good beyond the systems of good and bad. It is something to trust in. It is something vast, so vast that it exceeds small, human notions of like and dislike, positive and negative, this and that. I am a huge fan of Trungpa, and of this way of talking about dualism, because it seems to capture something with an efficiency of language, and something that is basically impossible to capture. Somehow, he does it, as many great teachers have.

Higher and lower do not exist as fixed, real categories, but they do have some meaning. The term "basic goodness" uses the word "good," so that's the same kind of thing. One way that TSK handles this dilemma is with the the three level description. First level things, such as words, knowing, time, whatever you like, is very caught up in dualism and limitations thereof. Second level stuff is less constricted, and there's a lot of questioning of limits, boundaries, and ideas. Some magic begins to arise. A lot can happen at the second level, and Tarthang even writes that spiritual breakthroughs or instances of things like deep intuition or special abilities can happen at this level. Any kind of development tends to be dualistic, though, still buying into good versus bad, so the third level untied this knot. At the third level, the differences between first and second, between openness and closed downness, between creativity and roboticism, are seen through. There's no need, at the that level, for effort to develop or improve things, and distinctions between wisdom and idiocy are seen to be lacking. We got here from a discussion about the use of language, specifically use of language in a more skillful way, according to the TSK model. The higher/lower model is useful at times, but the view of basic goodness, and the puzzle of the three levels are equally important.

Freedom with Positions and Conventions- We spend a lifetime finding our way through the crowded, chaotic marketplace of positioned ideas (I am a democrat because of this idea, based on this framework, and such evidence, or I am a republican for similar reasons) and conventions (I live my life his way, engage in these routines, speak this way, because I have selected from cultural lists of choices).

The obvious problem here is also a doorway to a solution. You cannot just abandon positions and say something like, "I am not political at all," because you are stil participating, in some way in politics, even if you don't have one party you strongly identify with. You have to have some ideas about the right way for government to treat people. You have some ideas about what project your local government should undertake. To avoid a position becomes a position anyway, so not choosing is no option. That's the thing about being alive. This goes for conventions too. Whether we go along quietly with the way things are done, or find angles to break out and do our own thing, we are still in the fight, still faced with how to be conventional or unconventional. Tarthang is saying that, with the growth of some wisdom, positions and conventions can become something that is less of a trap. They are a trap, for most of us, because we view them as either or propositions.

Either be political, or don't. Either believe this way, or that way. Be a normal person, or a weird person. Be a free spirit or a model citizen. Use your time efficiently or waste it with fun and recreation. The lists are built mostly on stupid black and white setups, and everyone knows, at some level, that those black and white choices are not nuanced enough to fit with the way the world works, and with the way we really want to live. So freedom means finding ways to not be bound by positions and conventions, but to use them creatively. This sounds a little bit like being dishonest or saying and doing whatever serves your purposes, and I don't want to suggest that. What I do want to suggest is that living creatively and with style is connected with not feeling controlled or limited to a small set of options, when it comes to words, actions, really anything. This is doing something different. This is another slogan, same idea, which is "there may be other options."

Don't get lost in words. They are like furniture, move them around to create functionality and beauty. I have presented a few visions of the fruition of the meditator's path, and what it looks like before we reach that. Remember the idea of knowledge not getting below the surface of language. This, along with the ideas about creativity, goodness, and freedom, is a way to gauge progress. If you're unsure about how you're doing when it comes to living with language, look to whether knowledge seems to be happening at a surface level, or going a little deeper.

Sanity

I believe I mentioned sanity near the beginning of this book. The essential slogan so Selfless Self Help is "Sanity for Oneself and Others." It's pretty clear. We need to become better people, less neurotic people for ourselves, for our own benefit, and for other people, to help them. I remember times from when I was a teenager, and my friends began maturing. One day, they would be a little bit sillier, more carefree and childish, and at some point, they seemed to change. They became adults. This was usually unpleasant, as I experienced it. I felt unsure of how to act around these newly minted, serious adults. Did they still laugh? Could we still hang out? Looking back now, it seems strange that I felt such a gulf between myself and my friends, considering how old I am now, and how much I've changed since that time. The people I thought of as so grown up then would probably seem less so now. Of course, they've changed too. Time didn't stop for them either.

There is an outer, or more obvious meaning to sanity for self and others, which, like I said, is about maturing. There is an inner meaning, too. The inner meaning is about the definition of sanity. To a meditator, becoming more sane does mean becoming more reasonable, kind, all the things you'd associate with maturity, but also becoming wiser in terms of nonduality. A sane meditator is someone who has worked on themselves, and has gotten some grasp of the meaning of nonduality for themselves. Trungpa Rinpoche talks about outer and inner authentic presence, and this is related. People, he writes, can exude a sense of presence just based on being "modest and decent and exertive." Then, inner authentic presence is the result of a more intense and precise process of training the mind and body, basically what we've been looking at this whole book. The only way to experience this is to try it, and see the changes, but of course, that takes time, and the changes can be subtle. Look at and spend a little time around older or more experience yogis. Then you can sense this kind of presence or being. It is naturally wholesome, intriguing, and sometimes a little scary, although the it is scarier at first, when it's less familiar. Let's go back to the quote about outer authentic presence, though, in full, because it's a good one.

There is an outer or ordinary sense of authentic presence that anyone can experience. If a person is modest and decent and exertive, he will begin to manifest some sense of good and wholesome being to those around him.

This is what people talk about when they say someone has a good energy, or they're easy to be around. It's a "vibe." I think it's important that the outer and inner versions of this are similar; it

290

means that the inner version is not that far off, or hard to imagine. If you want to know what a good meditator's energy is like, it's often like a heightened version of that pleasant sense of being that surrounds "modest, decent, exertive" people, and those qualities, modesty, decency, and exertion, are worth looking at, as well.

Sacred world is one in which the profound, sometimes strange truths of philosophy become apparent, or present themselves, in the visceral experiences of the world. At the same moment, this sacredness is supported by things like modesty and decency. I can't tell you how to live your life, or how to act, and certainly it's a nuanced issue, but I guess my point is that the beauty of the world is not separate from the virtuous life, or the life of trying to become a more and more virtuous person. The sense of these terms, modesty, decency, exertion, is, additionally, very down to earth, plain even. Entering sacred world does mean becoming a shaman, if that term can be understood in a modern sense. Still, shamanism does not mean, necessarily, doing weird drugs, dancing to drums, or having strange visions in nature. It doesn't mean those things are disallowed, exactly, but that shamanism, or being a yogi, which is the same thing, in this context, is very normal. It is a positive, heightened, charged kind of normalcy. Many great meditators have, in the recent and distant past, been lowly people, working menial jobs, or even being homeless. They did not appear cool or remarkable. They had incredibly profound inner lives. Some had magical abilities. Yet, they didn't show this to most people, and probably seemed not worth noticing, someone you'd pass on the street without a second thought. Charged normalcy is very different from conformity, so, again, I'm not snubbing my nose at people who do go wild, or dance, or even surround themselves with pretty crystals. Our journeys are our own, and subject to customization, and I think is even holds for people who are very orthodox. But the idea of special normalcy is not that the yogi must conform and fit in, while secretly going off to practice once a day. That's one way to do it. There are many. Normalcy, here, means that you can negotiate your own conformity, and wildness, and that this is significant in relation to being a mediator who lives in sacred world.

This lead into the slogan, "cultivate natural spiritual eccentricity." Most people are, I would venture, pretty eccentric, naturally. People are more flexible, open, and different than they seem. The cocoon is not just something that exists on a personal level. It also exists on larger levels: neighborhood, region, country, and so forth. When you begin to break through the layers of habituation and addiction, your life starts to slowly become more full of possibilities. This sounds like a cliche and it might be, but it is true. One reason we don't, so much of the time, don't keep the infinity of possibilities in mind is just that they are infinite, and it feels overwhelming or confusing to keep them in mind. So we tune them out. This just reinforces the walls of the cocoon. When those walls start to erode, and they are always wording a little bit, but we like to build them back up, when those walls start to really erode, and we let them, or encourage them, possibilities tune back in. The options come into relief. Part of the possibilities coming into relief is that people's natural eccentricities come out. I've found this to be true. You are free to be more eccentric and more normal, both are on the table. This is sanity for oneself and others. It is sanity for oneself because your mind has become a little more flexible, and your choices have expanded. It is sanity for others because when we grow, we naturally radiate this out to our community. Radiating an enlightened presence out to the community is a good thing.

Selfless Self Help

Languages

Language is a form of radiation, a form of radiating outwards. Very simply, if sanity for others is desirable, think of how much our language could change, and help others. Think about how much neurotic language is out there. Watch the news. Listen to the gossip and complaints of others. Look at how people treat each other poorly, small interactions, even if they're trying to find ways to connect or be polite, somehow it's hard to rouse the energy to compassionate. Think of how being around others whose thoughts are very densely negative, or anxious, or unbalanced is trying. You have to catch your breath after encounters like these. Living around people like this, which is not at all unusual, means a constant balancing act. That is a matter of language. When you feel someone else's unease, fear, or uprightness, you are not hearing their thoughts in some psychic way, probably, but you are tuning into something, some very faint radio station of thinking, and since thinking happens largely through a language process, the whole thing is a matter of words. Think of how much we could help our communities, our countries, by improving language skills. There is no sanity for self or other without language.

Rituals need language, even if it is just the language of a form and prescribed movements. In order to receive a mantra in Tibetan Buddhism, you must go through an initiation usually. The words of the mantra hold some power, and your mind needs to be tuned to connect with that power. Words are tricky. We might think that we can wield them using logic alone, but somehow there are layers of meaning and force to be worked through. Once we touch on to words, something amazing happens, and more often than not, things get out of hand, the electricity of them jolts us into other states of mind, other place, times, they move us. "I heard that if you hear the name of Milarepa [a famous Tibetan saint] you'll automatically become enlightened. I think I've heard it, so why am I not enlightened?""Yes, but did you really hear it?"

I chose to emphasize language because it allows me to talk a little bit about ritual practice, it allows me to talk about the way the mind works, and magic in a different way than before. Before, magic is something I talked about a tiny bit, mostly in the context of sense experiences, living in the world and having senses. This is one thing that is reclaimed through practice and joining a spiritual community: you reclaim, slowly, a sense of being firmly planted in the world. At high points, this can become psychedelic- your tea steaming in a mug can become entrancing. But usually it's not super dramatic, even when it's there, it does not stop your mind or pierce you entirely. It's just a feeling or a noticing of the wonder of simple perceptions. This is one kind of magic. Another kind involves going beyond, releasing, stretching past concepts. This can be done intellectually, as when you dissect a concept carefully, and begin to realize places where you were inaccurate, or new avenues to explore, but this is not so much how I learned, and not how I practice. I prefer less scientific approaches, here. The main goal is to unravel the mind so that our experience of what it is to have a mind, or to experience through mind changes. One way that I like is to work with language.

In John it says, the "the word was with God, and the word was God." From illuminated manuscripts, ornate Celtic designs, up through Arabic intricacy, advertising, and graffiti, words have fascinated for ages. They are hypnotic. People love words, so much that they build art out of them, get in huge arguments about the minuscule details of them, repeat them obsessively. Yet, we mostly skim over the surface, because we're so immersed in language, not really questioning it, or looking deeply at it. Strangely, it is powerful, everywhere, and functional, but the minute we try to pin it down or grasp it, this thing we call language wriggles away, mercurial.

Language is powerful, and it is everywhere. Although it is not the
only way, one thing I'd like to do here is offer some ideas about
how to transform language, and use language (as opposed to
presenting a theory about the nature of it, or what it means- these
things are currently beyond me, anyway, the use of words is a more
practical matter, and one I feel that I can actually honestly
comment on).

So that's one, I believe, honesty. This is a bedrock teaching in
Buddhism, and Christianity too. Tell the truth. Be honest with
yourself and others. I cannot claim to be totally honest and open,
but it something I work at all the time, and something to
contemplate all the time. Using language, as we think quietly, or as
we talk to friends and strangers, has to begin with honesty, and
honesty begins with being true to oneself. Without being true to
yourself, how could you express things in a genuine way to others?
The discipline of being honest is very challenging, and gives a
good, hard starting point for the alchemy of language. The alchemy
of language is not a matter of manipulation, gamesmanship, or
messing around. It is a real thing, and its foundation is honesty. To
put it another way, a lot of New Age garbage exists because people
aren't honest or hardheaded enough. They let imagination and

playfulness and wishfulness take over, in spite of honesty, and the result is a barfload of shiny crystals, silly necklaces, and books crammed full of greasy jargon webs.

Honest language starts off as a sense of common hearted simplicity, directness, but it need not end there, and playfulness, cleverness, don't need to be exiled. Play, actually is one thing a noted Buddhist teacher, Ngakchang Rinpoche, mentioned in an interview about language and the Buddhist teachings, an interview I'll be drawing on for the rest of this chapter. I'm using this interview to focus my discussion of this topic, because I respect the accomplishments and wisdom of this teacher, and because he also has some interesting ways of thinking about and using language (and that is, mind you, the English language, which is not the only one to use, but it is mine, and one I hope to use well). Ngakchang Rinpoche mentions play as one quality of language he tries to use when teaching; honesty is a foundation stone, but play is good too, perhaps keeping things from becoming overly formal or dry or boring.

Ngakchang mentions a few things: play, sensitivity to connotation, being poised in space, styles, and meaning. I'll go through these, and then, in addition, do a quick analysis of the language of various authors, both Buddhist and self improvement-oriented. Firstly, play. Talking about play is like talking about humor, it usually falls a little flat, just due to the seriousness of the discussion, but I'll try to avoid that. Play is worthwhile in terms of meaning, mostly. The kind of play with words that Ngakchang is talking about, a kind of lightness or sense of creativity, doesn't happen without there being a strong sense of meaning or meanings being conveyed. For whatever reason, over the last week, I've been making puns using Thai words and English words with my wife. My grasp of spoken Thai has gotten decent enough so that I can do this. My vocabulary is still extremely limited, but I'm slowly making progress. Playing with puns, double meanings, and so on, happens because meanings can be contrasted. I can't seem to remember any offhand right now, my memory does that, but let's say, for example, that I said something about eating beef, like "hew cow." The phrase "hew khao [similar sound]" in Thai means "I'm hungry," or, more literally, "I want food." Cow/beef, khao/cow, so you get it. It's a silly pun. It works on some level because the meanings intersect, and can interact with each other.

Language could be compared to many interdependent systems, a forest, a web, a network. Whenever words are used they play off of each and themselves, bringing up associations and shades of meaning. This is why word choice can be so difficult for a writer. One word carries thousands of years of connections. Then, it connects to other words. This is the play I'm trying to talk about. The sense of "play," though is also that it need not be so burdensome. It can be light. Writers and teachers try to express truth, in millions of different ways, but a sense of lightness makes it work better sometimes, and definitely makes it easier. To sum up, play means a sense of the interactions and senses around words, and using this with a little lightness and creativity. I just had he thought, too, that play can mean give, or flexibility, as in "the rope has some play in it," so that's there also. Definitions and discussions aren't set in marble, they have play.

This goes back to the very beginning. Think of spontaneity! You probably don't realize it, because we tend to overlook our own strengths, and because our minds move so quickly, but you've probably improvised many times today, and found many little solutions. Even lifting a heavy, awkward object means improvising and problem solving- finding the best grip, how to position your body, how to manage the balance of its weight, feeling if it is slippery or rough. Moving through space in a city or store is a constant improvised dance. If you look closely, you'll see many examples like this. Life is like this, it has play. With words, part of the big idea with play is that it is both practical and enjoyable to experience this action. We can't emphasize one more than the other, or it gets too trivial or too dull. Simultaneously, play involves meanings, and this is such a huge deal for people that we can never forget it.

I've already talked about sensitivity to connotation a little bit, as the connectedness of words and shades of meaning. If making something with language means playing, connotations are the shadows of that play. Sometimes it isn't necessary to pay much attention to them, but sometimes it is. If I'm creating something, or trying not to offend someone, or trying to explain something, connotations are important. Words are like suns. Their connotations, all the ways they've been used, the places they've been, are like the stars and planets. They hover around them. Their gravity affects each other.

Being poised in space is difficult to talk about. This is one place where words, as form, being to fight with their usages. Here are a few novice ideas about how to interpret this part of the teaching on language. First, think of space and energy, which are not separate from the masculine and feminine principles mentioned earlier in the book. Everything can be seen as space and energy. Looking at feelings this way can be especially helpful, and Pema actually writes about this age-old technique, feeling emotions as energy with direction, texture, movement. Anger can feel hot and complicated. Frustration is like anger, but with more resistance and a kind of shell around it. Clearly, the way I describe these things is personal, idiosyncratic and not scientific. You can do this for yourself, and that's what should be done. Both turning the mind to experience feelings in the body as energy and space at place, this, and overall experiencing the contrast and interaction of space and energy, are personal. There will be some ways your experience overlaps with those of others, some ways it won't, and this is acceptable. We're not trying to turn perceptions into equations or formulas. We're trying to have a precise yet artistic experience of reality. Looking at the interplay of negative space and forms in painting can be extremely valuable when it comes to energy/space. All forms of art can, and it probably depends a lot on which senses, sight, hearing etc, you connect with most easily (as far as which forms of art will most readily help you learn about this principle).

But, I don't know that I've actually addressed the application of the masculine and feminine principles to language. Ngakchang talked about words being poised in space. First, intuitively, you get some idea of what he means, and this is mostly likely the best idea of it, better than I could give you through explanations. Second, there is the word 'poised': so, not hanging in space, not just existing or being, but poised. There's the sense of existing in contrast to something surrounding, a background, and being light, agile, ready to move and dance or even attack. Poise suggests grace, self control in a fairly relaxed way, and a knowledge of how things should be done (a knowledge of decorum). This applies to both spoken and written language.

Style is not to hard, as opposed to the previous topics. You can find your style, and your styles, not just with your word, but in your life. There are many styles, which follow a basic pattern of a few, but manifest in a variety of interesting, surprising, and strange ways, person to person. You don't need to imitate a teacher or spiritual figure with your style, although I do think they provide some inspiration as far as what the limits and possibilities are. But, it could be your style, and we all know how uncomfortable it feels when either we or someone else is obviously trying to be something other than themselves. Style can be powerful, a way to get things done, and also fun.

Lastly, meaning. There is nothing I can say about this here. I think it is possible you have some ideas of your own. Now, a few words about the three authors I've been talking about throughout the

book, Pema, Trungpa, and Tarthang. Pema is the easiest to talk

about, and the hardest, in a way. Her language is simple and direct.

Not that she doesn't have a memorable turn of phrase here and

there, and she certainly has a sense of humor, but she is not playful

or strange in the way the other two are. Pema tells stories, usually

from her personal experiences. She gives instructions on how to

integrate meditation practice with life, and heart and emotions play

a big role in her teaching. It would be easy to sell her short,

because of her humble and ordinary style, but this would be a big

mistake. She is a powerful teacher, one who has touched millions

of people, especially those who wouldn't call themselves

Buddhists, meaning her impact has extended far beyond the

traditional monastic world she is a part of. A dedicated practitioner,

her words have weight not only because of their truth, but because

of excellent credentials as a meditator. I want to hold her up not

just as someone in contrast to Trungpa and Tarthang, but someone

who shows how to teach profound, brilliant wisdom in a

disarmingly simple style.

Trungpa, as he often does, presents obstacles and entices at the

same time. It is enticing to write about him, language-wise,

because there is so much to say. It is obstacle-ridden because there is so much to say, and what can be said seems to usually slide off the point, somehow; he is bulletproof, conceptually. Still, I hope that I can say a few decent things here. Saying not too much here will probably make it easier. I'm going to choose four qualities of his writing, somewhat at random based on what comes to mind, but also as someone who has studied him closely for years, so, not entirely at random. Metaphor, keywords, use of "we," and environment. First, metaphor.

This is one of the most obviously striking elements of his writing (and speech, since most of his "writing" is edited transcripts of teachings he gave). One of his students called his style of teaching and transmission "living metaphor." From one angle, he seemed to be saying that life was one metaphor after another, one layer over another of metaphor, or "symbolism." The cocoon I spent so much time on the first section is a metaphor, although it is easy to forget this once you've entered Trungpa's world. What begins as a metaphor becomes a keyword or catchphrase, and the original thing (the shell of an insect) becomes more or less forgotten in favor of the new meaning (a shell of habits, fear, aggression). Metaphor is at the heart of what language is and does. Metaphor allows for connections to be made, and for nets or strata of meaning to be created, invoked, or revealed. Many words connect to other words, associations, references to art and culture, and have many shades of meaning to them. In the way that metaphor stretches conventional definitions in order to give a new light to things, words always do this, in some way, just by virtue of being labels on a reality that is dynamic. It is a reality impossible to tie down, but language is a net. Metaphor, what we are calling metaphor, is a just a highlighted or intensified or artistic version of what language already is, which is to say that all language is metaphor. "Table" is symbolic just like "heart of gold" is symbolic. So Trungpa changes our relationship to language, and because language is married to thought, at this point (maybe not at some point in the distant, prehistoric past), he changes our relationship with thought. Finally, metaphor reminds you of intuition, and this function is often seen in art, but the Vidyadhara used it in his teaching as well, and we see it outside of art, too. When you hear a metaphor, you have to interpret, not based on scientific data or logical argument, but based on quick under the radar connections.

Metaphors become keywords, although they're not the only kind of keyword or jargon. I mentioned cocoon. Some others would be "personal,""possibilities," and "gentleness." These terms, along with a hundred or so others, appear again and again in this man's teachings. Because they show up over and over, in slightly

306

different circumstances, they both develop clear meanings and develop a mandala or association of nuances. They mean many things, all at once, grouped around a single theme. So, when used or invoked, they bring up, I think, all of those associations. In that way, they are both magical and very practical. The student or listener is guided towards remembering certain things by use of repetition (and, as a person who is used to the chaos of technology and noise, I don't find some styles of repetition in teaching palatable, so it helps that his style was a little confusing, complex, and very deep, I'm being reminded to remember things over and again, but the complexity and artfulness of it makes his memorization painless, fun even).

I have talked about Tarthang's language already, so what can I add to what's been said before? He has a depth nearing Trungpa's, but with more flamboyance, more noticeable artistry. Both T-word teachers could be seen as poets. If Chogyam is like a writer who is challenging, but rewarding, full of layered meanings and complexity, a modernist, maybe, Tarthang is like this, but more playful, more exuberant. (I'd almost compare Tarthang to a Beat poet, but I think he has more going on than most Beats, more to say. Maybe he's sort of a postmodernist, like Paul Auster- lots going on, lots of winks at the viewer.) All have their strengths and weaknesses. Some people will gravitate more to one than another. They all point out, in their own fashions, ways that language can be wielded as a weapon of enlightenment. It is well known, at this point, in some circles, that Trungpa's students began aping his speech at one time in their development. They copied his odd grammar and use of certain double-edged terms (like "it seems," or "particular'). It became clear, after not too long, that this was not the way to go, for students of the dharma. We can't steal from great teachers. It is tempting and unavoidable sometimes, as the words we absorb easily become our own, unconsciously, and everyone has their influences, and their anxiety of influence. True originality is a moving target, maybe the most difficult one ever, but something like it is possible. Then again, life is composed of tools. The pursuit of the genuine is extremely admirable, frighteningly admirable, but I must remind myself, too, again and again, that it's important to look at the results my language will have in time- it is a tool, and tools are there to be used for results.

The Toilet

Knowledge that reveals the luminosity of being bears within itself its own luminous shining. When we can inhabit such a world illuminated by such knowledge, we can act without fear or obstruction. (Tarthang Tulku, Dynamics of Time and Space)

The next slogan goes, "master your mind's energy, but still be able to flush the toilet." Here is how to look at it. You've addressed the entrapping properties of habits. You've become more spontaneous, and your life has begun to open up. You've looked at your own judgment and hypocrisy, and started to build a more allowing and honest relationship with your world, and its residents. By sitting consistently, maybe even doing a few retreats, your mind has become trained at slightly deeper levels, and the living experience of sense perceptions has changed. This all has contributed to an understanding, beyond just intellectual understanding, of sacredness. All of this is very good, and the point, but still, you have to be able to flush the toilet. You have to be able to drive safely, hold down a job, keep a fairly clean house, and be a good member of whatever community or communities you live in. The luminosity of being is wonderful, but it doesn't make it okay to forget about the details. Imagine a world in which everyone was meditating, but nobody took out the trash, or paid bills, or took care of their kids. Or, more likely, imagine a world where one group of elites meditated all the time, and another group took care of the practical details. It wouldn't work.

This approach is one of charged normalcy. The charged part, where you charge up through spiritual practice, has to be combined entirely with the normal part, if society is to function. I'm not, clearly, offering a clear vision of how society should work, or the role of meditators in society. I am suggesting, however, that meditators need to be good at being good neighbors where they live, and just good at living. That's probably a better way to look at it. We all have strengths and weaknesses. I may never become super organized or great at balancing a checkbook (so to speak, nobody uses check books anymore) but I can try to work on those things, and to become better at as many parts of life as possible.

Before I wrap this up, let's look back, momentarily, at habits, and the areas we started looking at early on. (Keeping in mind that I believe this is also a lifetime's work. Habit and spontaneity will always be worth touching in with.)

First, just think about a few problem patterns in your life right now. Where are the arguments and tension happening? Where do you feel trapped or stuck? Consider applying some different tactics there. Just as I write this, and think about it in my own life, I feel a small surge of fear, and I think that is a good thing, in a way, if not a pleasant one. It means something is there, and that space is opening up, energy is becoming liberated.

Think about some people you've judged lately (and maybe rightfully so, being judgmental can be very accurate sometimes, that is part of its energy oftentimes). What is being pointed out to you, about yourself?

Now, let's go back to the list we worked on in the beginning. Here it is, in case you've forgotten it.

Have a look at this list. Write down, or think about the answers.

As I look over the list myself, I can see that I still have work to do with almost all of of these areas. If all of them need work, for you, that's completely fine. Progress is usually gradual and slow. At the same time, I'm happy with the progress I've made, and how my life had changed just by applying a little pressure to these areas, and how the cocoon has less power in my life these days. Progress is gradual, and it should happen.

Think about number thirteen. It may be helpful to write these out, or just to think about it. There should be a number of sides, more than just two or three. I'd be very surprised if anyone has just two sides to their personality. The idea, with this, is not to become who you really want, exactly, because that might not be realistic. People seem to contain multitudes, and these facets also cycle through in fascinating ways. Some sides are neutral, some angelic, some demonic. Think of the more problematic or negative selves, the personalities or aspects where painful thoughts and emotions seem to occur the most frequently. I'm sure you've tried things in the past to cope with these, and, in fact, a lot of the work we've been doing has been this. I would encourage you to keep an open and flexible attitude with regard to there problem areas. Here, I'm suggesting this in terms of the personality itself, not just the habit pattern (and the basic idea is the same, but it's a very slightly different angle). Of course, no one of these personality displays, these personality presentations, is central. What I find interesting is that the negative ones, those associated with a lot of pain or angst, seem to magnetize a feeling of centrality. To use less odd lingo, it seems to be natural to assume the negative parts of e self are who we really are. I used to feel this so strongly when I'd get high, "this is who I really am."

It took me getting my life together and doing a lot of work before I realized that this was not true. Obviously, it is part of who I am, whether or not I ever go back to it. Still, it is not essentially central to who I am. When I realized this, I thought about all the other things I do, and all the other sides to my mind- musical, dreaming, intellectual, practical, food loving, artistic, and so on. It is insane to think that one part is the center, and this is the case whether you strongly identify with a negative aspect, or not. (I say this, but I also assume that most people, at some level, strongly identify with some negative aspect.)

I have reached no final realization with regards to this, and even if I had, I doubt I could transplant it into the reader's mind via this book. I have seen some encouraging progress, though, and so I am encouraging you, too. I am saying that this part of the process, looking at the self, is worth trying, and worth persevering with. Think, also, about the parts of the self you want to experience more, that you don't feel or see enough.

Selfless Self Help

Right now, my life is good, hard sometimes, but good. The intensity of anxiety and depression I felt at one time are gone. Many problems and painful feelings about myself are gone. The overall sense that I had to hide, and that living my life was not worth the huge effort I felt it took, that's much smaller. My life is so much more flexible now. My job is not perfect, but I have learned from it, and I also have learned how to work, and be an adult when it comes to that part of my life. I don't really do martial arts any more, although I'm thinking about getting back into it. It could be interesting, and there are actually a lot of teachers in my area. Maybe I will, maybe I won't. The main thing, for me, is that the initiatory process that started, more or less, with martial arts, and drugs, in my teens, has led somewhere. It has led me to a path that incorporates every part of life, and let's me live fully. I've been teaching the principles presented here in his book for about a year and a half. I would never have been able to do it well years ago. Now, things have changed. I did some teaching the past, and have slowly gotten used to it. It was not natural for me, for a long time, but I took it as a challenge, sometimes a rough one, and learned slowly how to talk in front of groups, works with classes, and so on. Teaching a meditation class has come naturally out of learning to teach English classes, and other regular classes.

Taking this route, teaching, has been very challenging and very interesting. I don't know how good I am at it, or if I'll continue. I hope that I will. One thing that has come out of it is a sense of who I am, or another side of my personality. I can say, now, with some honesty, that I am a meditation teacher. Part of this is that I feel compelled to behave better. When I'm driving, or taking to my wife, or at work, and I get upset, I remind myself that I am a meditation teacher. Over time, and it hasn't been that long, but still, over time, I've grown a little just by keeping this in mind. There have been so many teachers who have talked well, but have failed to be decent people in their personal lives, and I don't want to fall prey to this. So I try to be as decent, and kind as possible. No big breakthroughs yet, but I keep going! Even more than this, I try to reduce my own hypocrisy as much as I can. I want to be able to teach, but to do that, I have to be able to live and apply the teachings, so if I talk about patience, for example. I have to be, to some extent, patient. My life and what I teach others have to line up. This has been great training for me, and extremely difficult!

My life is good now. The silence is very powerful, and I am getting closer to it, slowly. I am grateful to all of my teachers. I thank you for reading this.

Selfless Self Help

The Meta-Religious Way

What I've presented in this book is an introduction to what I've been calling "meta-religion." A more practical or technical way of describing what I'm doing is by saying that my classes, Selfless Self Help, can serve as basic training for anyone intrigued by the idea of religion or spiritual life, which I consider to be the same. I don't usually offer anything so free form as to devolve into a loose discussion of what life should be, or what it means to be a good person, but I do think the basic structure of the course could be useful in many ways to people who identify themselves as Christian, Jewish, Hindu, and so on. The body/speech/mind setup, which is easy to see in the structure of the book, and is very Buddhist in a way, gets applied, along with an enthusiasm for seasons, for seasonal and natural cycles of practice. This includes the holidays. I feel that there are great amounts of energy at work during natural cycles, and this can be felt without too much trying. I believe that there are great amounts of energy at work during holidays, and this can also be felt. While living in Thailand, I nostalgically wanted to celebrate some sort of Christmas, but the main obstacle to doing this wasn't a lack of decorations, because you could actually find those, or a lack of Christmas trees, but a lack of general feeling, a lack of atmosphere (which has mostly to do with group energies localized in a place).

One twist, at the end, is that although I've been strongly emphasizing the negative possibilities of habits, as cocoon, and suggesting that becoming flexible is more important than having good habits, actually, at a point, this changes. Once you've loosened up for a while, developing and maintaining good habits is valuable. These become positive addictions. I see my practice this way, my going to the gym, washing dishes at night and in the morning, writing. Someday, I hope, and I have the feeling that my life was take the turn towards vast spontaneity, free from anxiety about little habits and the slow drip of building up virtue. For now, however, developing and maintaining habits is something I will practice. To say becoming good at both, the feminine principle as relaxing and being free, the masculine as organizing and accomplishing, is not enough, but it is something, a point.

If I continue to write on this subject, and teach on it, I hope to bring together people from many religious communities, along with the unaffiliated or skeptical, to sit and practice, and not only this, but to explore cycles of practice aligned with the natural order of things (such as the solstices, full moons, and so on). In terms of

317

writing, there is more to be said about this, but a lot of work will have to be done on my part to explore practices aimed at "weaving oneself in with the cosmic world."

The self help tradition, although looked down on by many, sometimes with good reason, still has its roots in the pagan/ classical and Christian lineages which shaped American culture and Western culture. Most self help books do not present as deep a tradition as do books on established, lively traditions such as Buddhism, or Judaism. Still, these popular works do get people to change their behavior and attitudes sometimes, and that is significant. These popular wisdom teachings do get people to practice. Think of Peale's instructions on using Bible verse like mantra. Think of affirmations, think of Tony Robbins' practice of starting the day with a set of specific "power questions." We don't need to say, imagine if this become one with the Buddhist tradition, or the yogi tradition. It is already happening. Those powerful, venerable schools of thought are already integrating, sometimes in subtle ways and sometimes in overt ways, into popular culture. Barring some kind of unforeseen and drastic change of course, this "infiltration of American karma," as Trungpa called it, will continue on, and the results are bound to be amazing-sometimes silly, sometimes awe-inspiring. One thing I'm driving at is that the standards for what constitutes self help will go up, and this will have less to do with scientific methods or data, more to do with the splendid mixing of traditions. As someone who has studied Buddhism and practiced its (often sly) methods, I have complained, mostly to myself, about how watered down modern yogic practice is, and modern New Age thinking. This is true. There is so much garbage out there. There probably always will be, because false spiritual practice gives safety and comfort where real practice gives peace, but not through imagined security or ego-calming reassurances. The real thing tends to be dangerous, not in a cult like way, but in the sense that people who take it on are tested continually, continually put on the spot, while being asked to maintain a strong mind and an entirely ethical lifestyle. So, the true path is not easy much of the time, and thus there will always be a market for the almost true path. However, and this could be overly optimistic on my part, we'll see. I do think that the power and sneakiness of actual wisdom teachings is such that they gradually work their way into every part of life. We are on the verge of a big change, an expansion of practice culture. The world has always been a melting pot, but right now we are seeing the growth of not just Asian culture worldwide, but the growth of wisdom culture here at home. I am not saying I am any significant part of this, probably this book will never get published, but I am saying that

Selfless Self Help

people do crave wisdom, sometimes looking at strong sources,
sometimes weak. The strength of said sources will be, in the near
future, being upgraded. I am looking forward to this.

Acknowledgements

I'd like to thank my wife, for her support and patience. I cannot express how indebted I am to my lama for his teachings, and his giving access to various practices, which he did generously and with kindness. I would also like to thank my various writing teachers. Finally, the meditation teachers who have guided me over the years, some of whom I met briefly, some of whom worked with me for longer: Eric Spiegel, Agness Au, Ethan Nicthern, Jeff Grow, and Joyce Haydock. I apologize for anyone I've thoughtlessly left off this list.

Selfless Self Help

Notes

[1] In this work, "pain" is more or less synonymous with the Buddhist use of the term suffering (dukha). Reading over this, I wonder where we can separate out meaning from pain. These two intertwine.

[2] Stubbornness is one of the most interesting things to me these days. Isn't there some just-below-the-surface mental action going on when we are stubborn about many things? A lot of times, I think people are stubborn for reasons they don't understand, but feel; stubbornness is a strategy for achieving half conscious future goals, and positioning ourselves. It can, of course, just be a way to seal ourselves off or protect against trying new and different things, a cocoon, but sometimes it is not that.

[3] Many so-called seekers will run from anything labeled religion, largely because it seems like too much of a commitment. I am not a fan of this approach, because ego or a sense of separate self is usually what makes the choices, for a "spiritual" type, as far as what gets adopted, and what parts of a given system get thrown out or avoided. So, it's about avoidance. The real path is about commitment, not immediately, but eventually, and finding some tradition means, for most, religion. I include Buddhism as one of these religions. Sadly, some people would argue that Buddhism is not a religion, but they would be hard pressed to explain philosophical texts, ethical rules, terminology, rituals and specialized garb, all of which tend to go along with religion.

[4] Or language. Maybe energy-language. That seems too academic or pretentious. At this point, the last of those three is somewhat nebulous.

[5] Yes, obviously Trungpa did not invent the term, and explicating the history of the term in general, Trungpa's usage, and modern understandings of it would take another book, but the idea here is that the self is not necessarily real in the ways people normally like to think it is.

[6] Later, I'll go into a cursory analysis of some actual self help writing. At some point, it would amazing to do a detailed and wide-ranging analysis of various works/authors, but that is beyond the scope of this book, which, then, assumes some familiarity with the genre.

[7] Frequency and making social/work life difficult are markers of addiction, but focus is, I think, the main one. If you are able to use some substance, but not worry or think too much about it during your day, then this is a good sign. If it becomes too central, especially to the detriment of one's ability to pay attention to others, this is a bad sign.

[8] I wish I could express this point in a more simply nuanced way. Most people are hardly spontaneous at all, and this needs to be transformed, worked through. At the same time, habits are needed, up to a point. (That point being enlightenment.) They are needed to help organize, and to allow us to help ourselves and others. To attempt to simplify or sum up: total spontaneity eventually, positive habits up to then. Along the way, plenty of mixing things up and trying new stuff.

[9] Actually, holidays have become a significant part of my practice. I enjoy them, if I can, and see them as part of the sacred calendar which shapes my year.

[10] Roboticism is a two-fold problem. First, it makes one less present. Second, it makes one less responsive. As to the first point, without presence, we don't truly live or experience the senses. Whatever tradition appeals, living is the goal. As to the second point, spontaneity means, in part, becoming more responsive to our world.

[11] Basically, siddhis are something you shouldn't get too into. They develop naturally over time, given the right circumstances. There are more important things to work at "getting," like bodhicitta, concentration, and bliss.

[12] Which is, in a way, a very strange thing to say in a book. Think of it this way. The book is here to encourage people to get out there and learn practices, then apply them. I don't imagine the ideas or path in this book are particularly important or groundbreaking. It's sort of like an exercise book that doesn't have that many things to say, just, basically, go out there and exercise, it's good for you. And don't confuse having read books about exercise with actually having worked out. You don't get to look like Mr. Universe by reading about lifting weights.

Selfless Self Help

13 There were other metaphors used too. "Entering" as a physical technique meant closing distance and positioning oneself, but could also have something to do, as symbol, with going bravely into some situation, not flinching or turning away. "Blending" as a physical technique meant coordinating with an attack so that you moved in a smooth, connected way with your partner (not a way that would immediately stop or oppose their attack). As a symbol, blending had something to do with going with the flow, connecting to an outside force of some kind and perhaps redirecting, but not opposing or clashing.

14 Ok, this is an important balance or contrast. Self improvement doesn't mean becoming someone other than yourself. Sometimes people will go through drastic changes in life, become unrecognizable to friends and family, sometimes due to big surprises, illness, and so forth. However, this is not how most people change, for most, it's gradual and slow. Also, very logical people don't usually become focused on emotion. Very sensitive people don't usually become utterly stable and thick skinned. Within your normal range of being, changes happen, but it's neither healthy nor realistic to hope for a total shift. That kind of shift within the range of your being can be drastic in its own way, it just isn't a matter of becoming some sort of ideal.

15 Actual self help has different takes on this issue, the issue of compassion, and working with others/the world. Robbins has "contribution" as one of his main drives or ways to get value out of life. Richardson suggests, I think, that helping others is assumed to be good. That's what gets people to the point at which they need to reassess, find ways to institute "self-care," that they've been putting some much time and energy into caring for others or paying attention to others. These are only two approaches. There are many more. Some focus more on the self, assuming it to be part of society (and thus, society is the area in which compassion is played out). Some incorporate compassion more directly, showing ways to get along, and achieve goals without harming others (too much).

16 It might seem bizarre to have this as a goal, especially for someone who takes life seriously, not being clumsy. Think of it this way: I see becoming more coordinated as something general, a general learning curve. Becoming more together, and more able to respond well in a given moment, are physical and mental, and these two are always connected.

17 Of course, contemplating what meaing is could be interesting.

324